RENAL DIET COOKBOOK FOR BEGINNERS

1500-Day Easy & Tasty Low Potassium, Sodium and Phosphorus Recipes for Your Kidney Health. Live Healthier without Sacrificing Taste. Includes 30-Day Meal Plan

Melissa Jordon

ISBN: 979-8359279901
10 9 8 7 6 5 4 3 2 1

BONUS

ANTI-INFLAMMATORY COOKBOOK FOR BEGINNERS

1200 Days of Simple Recipes to Heal the Immune System, Live Healthy and Reduce your Body Inflammation

MELISSA JORDON

THIS BOOK INCLUDES A
FREE BONUS

The "Anti-Inflammatory cookbook for beginners" is **100% FREE**, and all you need to get it is a name and an email address. **It's super simple !**

TO DOWNLOAD THE BONUS SCAN
THE QR CODE BELOW OR GO TO

https://melissajordon.me/bonus-rd/

SCAN ME

MELISSA JORDON
— *collection* —

Table of Contents

Introduction

What Is Renal Diet?

Every person is different, and everyone has different nutrients they will need to monitor with CKD. You may be at the same stage of CKD as someone but have completely different dietary needs depending on your body and your overall condition.

The Chronic Kidney Disease (CKD) diet requires you, your healthcare practitioner, and hopefully a dietitian to monitor your labs and progress to ensure you follow an appropriate diet. While it may be awesome to think about all the different components, the diet is manageable if you have the proper tools & guidance. Reading this book is a great sign that you are on the right path. You may feel overwhelmed or think that this diet is going to be terrible, but I promise you there are plenty of tasty recipes that can be created on a renal diet.

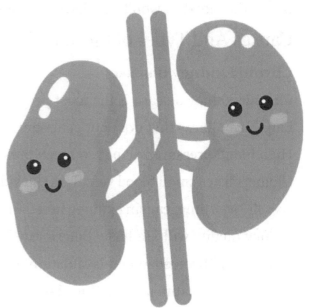

The renal diet includes a variety of whole grains, appropriate proteins, plenty of fruits and vegetables, and flavorful and fun seasoning and spices. Certain nutrients that people with CKD may need to watch out for include but are not limited to, potassium, protein, phosphorus, and sodium. While these nutrients are important to monitor depending on your needs, it's also good to note that there are many foods you can incorporate into your diet that are tasty as well as nutritious and good for your body.

What Is Kidney Disease?

The kidneys are two fist-sized organs at the base of the rib cage. For either hand of the spine, there is a kidney.

Kidneys are essential for a safe body. They mostly remove waste material, excess water, and other impurities from the bloodstream. Toxins are retained in the bladder and eliminated by urination. The kidneys also regulate the body's pH, sodium, and potassium. They make hormones that monitor red blood cell

formation and manage blood pressure. Even a type of vitamin D that the kidneys activate aids calcium absorption.

Kidney disease affects millions of people in the US. It happens as the kidneys become weak and sometimes unable to work correctly. Diabetes, hypertension, and various other chronic (long-term) disorders may also trigger harm. Kidney disease may result in brittle bones, nerve damage, and malnutrition, among other issues.

Your kidneys can stop functioning entirely if the disease progresses. This suggests that dialysis would be needed to carry out the kidney's operation. Dialysis is a procedure that uses a pump to clean and purify the blood. It won't heal kidney failure, so it will help you live longer.

Causes And Types of Kidney Disease?

Chronic kidney disease

Chronic kidney disease is the most prevalent form of kidney disease. A chronic kidney disorder is a long-term illness that does not get better. High blood pressure is a general factor.

High blood pressure will put so much pressure on the glomeruli in the kidneys, causing them to fail. Glomeruli are small blood vessels in the kidneys that clean the blood. The added strain destroys these vessels over time, causing kidney function to deteriorate.

Kidney quality will gradually deteriorate because the kidneys cannot function properly or correctly. Dialysis will be needed in this situation. Dialysis removes excess fat and waste from the bloodstream. Dialysis is a treatment for kidney failure, although it is not a remedy. Depending on the situation, a kidney transplant might be an alternative.

Diabetic nephropathy is a common complication of diabetes. Diabetes is a category of illnesses characterized by elevated blood sugar levels. Over time, the high

sugar content in the blood affects the blood vessels in the kidneys. This indicates that the kidneys are unable to cleanse the blood adequately. When your body is overwhelmed with chemicals, kidney failure may occur.

Kidney stones

Another common kidney condition is kidney stones. They create stable masses as minerals and other compounds in the blood crystallize in the kidneys (gravel). The body usually passes kidney stones through urination. Kidney stones may be excruciatingly painful, but they seldom trigger serious complications.

Glomerulonephritis

Glomerulonephritis is a condition under which the glomeruli become inflamed. Glomeruli are tiny blood-filtering devices found within the kidneys. Infections, medications, and congenital disabilities may all induce glomerulonephritis. It usually improves on its own.

Polycystic disease of the kidney

Polycystic kidney disease is inherited when the kidneys develop multiple cysts (tiny fluid sacs). These cysts can cause kidney failure by interfering with kidney function. (It's worth noting that specific kidney cysts are reasonably frequent and almost always benign.) Polycystic kidney disorder, on the other hand, is a different, more debilitating condition).

Urinary tract infections

UTIs are bacterial diseases of the urinary tract, which may affect any portion of the body. The most prevalent infections are those of the bladder and urethra. They are readily treatable and rarely result in further health issues. These infections will spread to the kidneys, which trigger kidney failure if not managed.

Why Sodium, Potassium and Phosphorus Are So Critical

a. *Sodium And Its Role in The Body*

A renal patient must reduce daily sodium and potassium intake to keep their kidney at rest. Sodium and salt are not interchangeable. People believe that salt is the only grocery item containing sodium, but other natural foods are high in sodium. Salt is a mixture of chloride and sodium. Canned foods and processed foods have a large amount of sodium in them.

Our body has three significant electrolytes, sodium, potassium, and chloride. Sodium regulates blood vessels and blood pressure, muscle contraction, nerve function, and acid balance in the blood and keeps the balance of fluid in the body! The kidney usually excretes the toxin in our body, but a damaged kidney cannot eliminate the extra sodium in our body.

So, when a renal patient consumes too much sodium, it gets stored in the blood vessels and bloodstream. This storage of sodium can lead to feeling thirsty all the time. It is a bit problematic as kidney patients must limit their fluid intake. It can cause edema, high blood pressure, breathlessness, and even heart failure. So, renal patient must always limit their sodium intake. The average limit is 150 mg per snack and 400 mg per meal.

Patients who struggle with kidney health issues, go through kidney dialysis and have renal impairments need to undergo medical treatment and change their eating habits and lifestyle to improve the situation.

The first thing to changing your lifestyle is knowing how your kidney functions and how different foods can trigger different kidney function reactions. Certain nutrients affect your kidney directly. Nutrients like sodium, protein, phosphate, and potassium are the risky ones. You cannot omit them altogether from your diet, but you need to limit or minimize their intake as much as possible. You cannot remove essential nutrients like protein from your diet, but you need to count how much protein you have daily. Maintaining balance in your muscles and maintaining a good functioning kidney is essential.

A profound change in kidney patients measures how much fluid they drink. It is a crucial change in every kidney patient, and you must adapt to this new eating habit. Too much water or any other form of liquid can disrupt your kidney function. How much fluid you can consume depends on the condition of your kidney.

b. *Potassium And Its Role in The Body*

Potassium maintains the balance of electrolytes and fluid in our bloodstream. It also regulates our heartbeat and contributes to our muscle function. You can find potassium in many fruits, vegetables, and meat. Besides, it also exists in our bodies. A healthy kidney keeps the required potassium in our body and removes the excess through urine.

A damaged kidney is not capable of removing potassium anymore. Hyperkalemia is a condition when you have too much potassium in the blood. Hyperkalemia can cause a slow pulse, weak muscles, irregular heart rate, heart attack, and death.

To control your daily potassium intake, count every ingredient's potassium level. It would help to consult a renal expert dietitian, as they know which ingredient would work best for your condition. Food like avocado, beans, spinach, fish, bananas, and potatoes are very high in potassium. Even if you eat these ingredients, try to divide the serving in half and eat a small one.

Do not eat these high-potassium ingredients every single day. There are many low-potassium foods available, so pick them when you make your meal plan. Fresh ingredients are always better than frozen kind. To keep track of your potassium intake throughout the day, keep a personal food journal where you can input everything and reflect when you need to.

c. *Phosphorus And Its Role in The Body*

Phosphorous contributes to keeping our bones healthy and developing them. Phosphorous helps in muscle movement and develops connective tissue and organs. When we eat phosphorous food, the small intestines store it to build our bones. A well-functioning kidney can eliminate the extra phosphorous in the body, but a damaged one cannot do so. So renal patients must watch how much phosphorous they are consuming.

Though phosphorous helps develop bones, it can also weaken them by extracting calcium if too much phosphorous is consumed. The calcium removed from the bones gets deposited in blood vessels, the heart, eyes, and lungs, causing severe health problems.

The proper knowledge of high-phosphorous food is required to balance phosphorous for a renal patient. Red meat, milk, fast foods like burgers, pizzas, fries, fizzy drinks that are colored, and canned fish and seeds are relatively high in phosphorous.

Packaged food or canned food also, is high in phosphorous. Therefore, read the labels before purchasing canned goods from the supermarket.

Phosphorous binders are an excellent way to keep your phosphorous intake to a minimum. If you ask your dietitian, they will give you an excellent phosphorous binder, which you can follow to track how much you can and should consume.

Benefits of Renal Diet

a. *How Eating Well Can Make a Difference*

The renal diet focuses primarily on supporting kidney health because, in doing so, you'll improve many other aspects of your health, as well. It can also be customized to fit all levels of kidney disease, from early stages and minor infections to more significant renal impairment and dialysis. Preventing the later stages is the main goal, though reaching this stage can still be treated carefully considering your dietary choices. In addition to medical treatment, the diet provides a way to gain control over your health and progression. It can mean the difference between complete renal failure and a manageable chronic condition, where you can lead a regular, enjoyable life despite having kidney issues.

b. *Eating Well Is a Natural and Medicine-Free Way to Help Your Kidneys*

Whether or not the medication is a part of your treatment plan, your diet plays a significant role in the health of your kidneys. Some herbs and vitamins can boost the medicinal properties found in foods and give your kidneys additional support while limiting other ingredients, which, in excess, can lead to complete renal failure if there are already signs of kidney impairment. Your kidneys thrive on fresh, unprocessed foods that make it easier for your body to break down, digest, and process nutrients. Choosing natural options also eliminates or reduces the amount of sodium and refined sugars you consume, so you don't have to continuously monitor how many grams of salt or sugar is in your foods.

If you have limited access to fresh fruits or vegetables, choose frozen as the next best option, as they will have retained all or most nutrients in their original state. Canned vegetables and fruits are often processed, though these can be added when no other options are available.

To reduce the amount of sodium they contain, rinse canned vegetables in the water at least twice before adding them to your meal or dish.

Canned fruit is often preserved in a thick or sugary syrup, which should be drained and rinsed before serving to reduce the sugar content. Always read the package's ingredients or can before you consider adding it to your grocery cart, and only choose these options where fresh or frozen selections are unavailable.

Unless directed by a physician or medical specialist, don't reduce or stop taking medication for your kidneys, even if there are significant improvements to your health due to dietary changes and/or medical improvements and an increased kidney function is noted. While diet should be a central part of your lifestyle, keep the medication as part of this treatment goal just the same. Any sudden or significant changes in your treatment plan can thwart any progress made and may cause further damage in the long term. Consider your food and meal choices in the renal diet as part of a whole, including exercise, medical treatment(s), and living well.

Shopping List

Many foods work well within the renal diet. Once you see the available variety, it will not seem as restrictive or difficult to follow. The key is to focus on foods with a high level of nutrients, which makes it easier for the kidneys to process the waste by not adding too much that the body needs to discard. Balance is a major factor in maintaining and improving long-term renal function.

a. *Foods To Eat*

Garlic: An excellent, vitamin-rich food for the immune system, garlic is a tasty substitute for salt in various dishes. It is a significant source of vitamin C and B6 while aiding the kidneys in ridding the body of unwanted toxins. It's a great and healthy way to add flavor to skillet meals, pasta, soups, and stews.

Berries: All berries are considered a good renal diet food due to their high level of fiber, antioxidants, and delicious taste, making them an easy option to include as a light snack or as an ingredient in smoothies, salads, and light desserts. Just one handful of blueberries can provide almost one day's vitamin C requirement and a boost of fiber, which is good for weight loss and maintenance.

Bell Peppers: Flavorful and easy to enjoy, raw and cooked; bell peppers offer a good source of vitamin C, vitamin A, and fiber. Along with other kidney-friendly foods, they make detoxification much easier while boosting your body's nutrient level to prevent further health conditions and reduce deficiencies.

Onions: This nutritious and tasty vegetable is excellent as a companion to garlic in many dishes or on its own. Like garlic, onions can provide flavor as an alternative to salt and provide a good source of vitamin C, vitamin B, manganese, and fiber. Adding just one-quarter or half of the onion is often enough for most meals because of its strong and pungent flavor.

Macadamia Nuts: If you enjoy nuts and seeds as snacks, you may learn that many contain high amounts of phosphorus and should be avoided or limited as much as possible. Fortunately, macadamia nuts are easier to digest and process, as they contain much lower amounts of phosphorus and make an excellent substitute for other nuts. They are a good source of other nutrients, such as vitamin B, copper, manganese, iron, and healthy fats.

Pineapple: Unlike other fruits that are high in potassium, pineapple is an option that can be enjoyed more often than bananas and kiwis. Citrus fruits are also generally high in potassium, so if you find yourself craving an orange or grapefruit, choose pineapple instead. In addition to providing high levels of vitamin B and fiber, pineapples can reduce inflammation thanks to an enzyme called bromelain.

Mushrooms: In general, mushrooms are a safe and healthy option for the renal diet, especially the shiitake variety, which is high in nutrients such as selenium, vitamin B, and manganese. They contain a moderate amount of plant-based protein, which is easier for your body to digest and use than animal proteins. Due to their texture and pleasant flavor, Shiitake and Portobello mushrooms are often used in vegan diets as a meat substitute.

b. Foods to Avoid

Eating restrictions might be different depending on your level of kidney disease. If you are in the early stages of kidney disease, you may have different restrictions than those in the end stage of renal disease or kidney failure. In contrast, people with an end-stage renal disease requiring dialysis will face different eating restrictions. Let's discuss some foods to avoid while on the renal diet.

Dark-Colored Colas contain calories, sugar, phosphorus, etc. They contain phosphorus to enhance flavor, increase its life, and avoid discoloration, which can be found in a product's ingredient list. This addition of phosphorus varies depending on the type of cola. Mostly, dark-colored colas contain 50–100 mg in a 200-ml serving. Therefore, dark colas should be avoided on a renal diet.

Avocados are a source of many nutritious characteristics and strong fats, fiber, and antioxidants. Individuals suffering from kidney disease should avoid them because they are rich in potassium. One hundred fifty grams of an avocado provides a whopping 727 mg of potassium. Therefore, avocados, including guacamole, must be avoided on a renal diet, especially if you are on parole to watch your potassium intake.

Canned Foods, including soups, vegetables, and beans, are low in cost but contain high amounts of sodium due to the addition of salt to increase their life. Due to this amount of sodium in canned goods, it is better for people with kidney disease to avoid consumption. Opt for lower-sodium content with the label "no salt added." One more way is to drain or rinse canned foods, such as canned beans and tuna, which could decrease sodium by 33–80%, depending on the product.

Brown Rice is a whole grain containing a higher concentration of potassium and phosphorus than its white rice counterpart. One cup of already-cooked brown rice possesses about 150 mg of phosphorus and 154 mg of potassium, whereas one cup of already-cooked white rice has about 69 mg of phosphorus and 54 mg of potassium. Bulgur, buckwheat, pearled barley, and couscous are equally beneficial, low-phosphorus options and might be a good alternative instead of brown rice.

Bananas are high in potassium content, low in sodium, and provide 422 mg of potassium per banana. It might disturb your balanced potassium intake to 2,000 mg if a banana is a daily staple.

Whole-Wheat Bread may harm individuals with kidney disease. But for healthy individuals, it is recommended over refined, white flour bread. White bread is recommended instead of whole-wheat varieties for individuals with kidney disease because it has phosphorus and potassium; if you add more bran and whole grains to the bread, phosphorus and potassium increase.

Oranges and orange juice are enriched with vitamin C content and potassium. One hundred eighty-four grams provides 333 mg of potassium and 473 mg in one cup of orange juice. With these calculations, they must be avoided or used in a limited amount while being on a renal diet. Other oranges and orange juice alternatives are apples, grapes, and their cinder or juices, as they contain low potassium content.

Potatoes and sweet potatoes are potassium-rich vegetables; 156 g contains 610 mg of potassium, whereas 114 g contains 541 mg of potassium, which is relatively high. Some high-potassium foods, like potatoes and sweet potatoes, could also be soaked or leached to lessen the concentration of potassium contents. Cut them into small and thin pieces and boil those for at least 10 minutes can reduce the potassium content by about 50%. Potatoes soaked in a wide pot of water for as low as four hours before cooking could possess even less potassium content than those not soaked before cooking. This is known as "potassium leaching" or the "double cook direction."

Snack Foods like pretzels, chips, and crackers are foods that lack nutrients and are much higher in salt. It is very easy to take above the suggested portion, which leads to an even greater salt intake than planned. If chips are made from potatoes, they will also contain a significant amount of potassium.

If you are suffering or living with kidney disease, reducing your potassium, phosphorus, and sodium intake is essential to managing and tackling the disease. The foods with high potassium, high sodium, and high-phosphorus content listed above should always be limited or avoided. These restrictions and nutrient intakes may differ depending on the level of damage to your kidneys. Following a renal diet might be a daunting procedure and a restrictive one most of the time. But, working with your physician and nutrition specialist, and a renal dietitian can assist you in formulating a renal diet specific to your individual needs.

FAQs

These are some of the most common questions that should clarify your many questions about what the renal diet represents and what it represents.

a. *What Is the Renal Diet Based on?*

The renal diet is a diet plan that restricts the group of foods that may cause damage to the damaged kidney system and kidneys. The main purpose of the diet is to help patients who have been diagnosed with certain kidney diseases to lead a healthier lifestyle so that they can manually regulate the presence of sodium, potassium, water, and waste, which healthy kidneys should produce, and the kidneys to regulate so the kidney function is normal. The renal diet is based on the introduction of foods that are low in sodium and potassium.

b. *Can I Use Meat Substitutes for Protein Sources?*

Patients with kidney disease that dislike or don't consume meat for different reasons may find a valuable dose of daily protein intake through several alternatives. Even though low protein consumption is recommended when on a renal diet, you need to ensure that you are not neglecting your body's need for protein. That is how renal patients who avoid eating meat need to find ways to take protein in a daily diet in recommended doses. For instance, instead of meat, you can turn to an animal-based protein found in cheese and eggs if you can't eat even small portions of meat. Since only low-sodium and low-potassium cheese is allowed, find suitable alternatives if you want to include cheese in your diet. Additionally, you need to talk to your doctor about the number of eggs and milk you are allowed to have daily and weekly. Moreover, you can use egg substitutes, and protein shakes mixed with fruit suitable for your condition and your diet regimen.

c. Why Is Alcohol on the Don't List of the Renal Diet?

Alcohol like wine and beer might be consumed moderately if allowed by your doctor. However, the general recommendation regarding alcohol regarding your renal diet and the well-being of your renal functions is to avoid alcohol at all costs. Alcohol may increase your blood pressure, help you gain weight and increase the levels of blood sugar in your body. Additionally, alcohol introduces more toxic waste to your body for your kidneys to work against, which may bring more damage to your kidneys while also potentially damaging your liver and pancreas. On top of these risks when consuming alcohol, one of the main reasons alcohol should be out of your range is that alcohol shouldn't be mixed with medications you are taking for your kidney condition.

d. Should I Lower My Liquid Intake on a Renal Diet?

The renal diet recommends the reduction of liquid as one of the effective ways to help your kidneys and improve your renal function since damaged kidneys struggle with removing excess water from your organism when liquid consumption is increased and above normal. However, only reduce your liquid intake if your doctor prescribes it, as an unnecessary liquid reduction may cause more problems to your body and health. Avoid sugar-packed drinks and sodas when it comes to beverages rather than water.

e. What Is Low and What Is Considered High Potassium in Food?

Potassium levels vary from one food product to another, while some store-bought groceries with nutrition labels won't even list potassium—that does not mean that the food product contains no potassium; it only means that the manufacturer didn't consider that listing this mineral is essential. You can always research potassium levels in almost any food you buy, and consuming low potassium is around 40 mg. In comparison, very high potassium levels are considered to be above 500 mg per serving, representing a concentration of 14% per portion.

Unless your doctor advises otherwise, you should lower your potassium intake to a minimum for the best results with a renal diet. However, you should remember that potassium is one of the essential minerals your body needs, so you shouldn't completely neglect the consumption of potassium through food.

f. Should I Take Vitamins and Herbal Supplements While on a Renal Diet?

People with chronic kidney disease may lack some essential vitamins that are categorized as water-soluble. In contrast, kidney patients that have dialysis treatment may lack these vitamins, such as groups of vitamin B. Other vitamins may also be lacking, regardless of the diversity in your diet. Even though you are eating enough healthy food, it should provide your body with all the nutrients it needs for proper functioning. However, we do not recommend taking any herbal or vitamin supplements when on a renal diet unless prescribed by your doctor. Your doctor may accurately prescribe additional doses of vitamins in the form of supplements based on your blood test results and deeper knowledge of your health condition and disease state. Do not take any supplements yourself, and do not consult a doctor.

g. What Can I Do About My Low Appetite?

Low appetite and inability to consume food regularly are common side effects for patients with kidney problems. This is the case because your kidneys struggle to eject all the waste build-up in your body. This state may cause a loss of appetite in the long run, which is not good for your body. When you are not introducing nutrients to your organism, your body needs to find another source of nutrients, drawing build-up nutrients from reserves and first "eating out" fat reserves in your body, then getting to your muscles.

You need to eat to prevent muscle loss and further damage to your health; however, eating with a poor appetite may seem like a mission impossible. Even in difficult times, you can take some measures to improve and increase your appetite.

• Try setting up an eating schedule for yourself and eat smaller portions packed with calories so that you can have as much energy and nutrients even though smaller portions of food when your appetite is lower. Try not to miss out on any scheduled meal that you have set up for yourself

• Fresh air and physical activity such as swimming, cycling, or even taking a walk may wake up your appetite and improve it

• When on low appetite, try snacking on healthy snacks and eat more frequently in smaller portions

• Make sure that your meals, even though small, have enough proteins and calories so you would prevent muscle loss and have the needed energy

• Eating your favorite food may work benevolently to improve your appetite. Make sure that the food you like eating is low in potassium and sodium

• Soups with added meat, such as ground beef or chicken, may be a great choice for you when you are having problems with eating, as you will be able to introduce your body to essential nutrients through a light meal that you might be able to eat more easily than it would be the case with solid food

• Add eggs and low-sodium cheese to salads when on low appetite to make sure that you are getting the nutrients you need even in case of poor appetite

h. Can I Eat Whole Grains and Nuts on a Renal Diet?

The renal diet advises caution when it comes to the consumption of whole grains and nuts, as these food groups have high concentrations of potassium. During checkups on your potassium levels as tested by your doctor, ask your physician whether you are allowed to eat whole grains and nuts. Patients who have just had a successful kidney transplant are recommended to have whole grains, nuts, and seeds and to increase protein consumption to encourage tissue repair, as well as beans and lentils, which are normally not the first food groups recommended in a renal diet.

i. Does the Renal Diet Work on Slowing Down the Progression of Chronic Kidney Diseases?

Even in case you are in the third stage of chronic kidney disease, the renal diet can help you improve your health as this diet is designed to improve the overall function of the renal system and kidneys, preventing further damage to your vital organs. However, the renal diet may not be as effective if your lifestyle does not complement the effects of a healthy diet that the renal dietary program represents. You must also improve your lifestyle to get the most out of the renal diet.

Besides eating healthy food as suggested in our grocery lists, you also need to introduce some physical activities to your everyday routine. It will be enough to jog, walk, hike, cycle, or swim, and be physically active for at least an hour a day or more if your health and physical constitution allow it. If you are overweight, you should reduce the excess kilograms because this will help your recovery and benefit your health. If you are having problems with blood sugar levels, presuming that the sugar levels in your blood are too high, cut on white flour and sugar. Stay hydrated and drink water instead of other beverages.

j. What Are Common Dietary Restrictions in a Renal Diet?

The renal diet prescribes recommended restriction of potassium and sodium as damaged kidneys are having problems leveling these minerals in your body. When having increased potassium and sodium levels, even though these minerals are essential for your health and overall well-being, more damage can be brought to your renal system. Aside from recommending a low potassium and sodium intake, the renal diet promotes decreased phosphorus consumption.

You may feel at the beginning of the renal diet that there are too many restrictions and that these food "bans" are too difficult to follow up with; however, you can talk to your doctor about the recommended dosage of sodium and potassium through your daily diet based on your health condition.

Hopefully, any doubts you might have had about the renal diet are now clear. In contrast, you have learned more about the positive effects this dietary regimen should have on your renal health with the ultimate goal of stopping the progression of your chronic kidney disease.

We have already emphasized how important it is for your health to cut down on potassium and sodium; however, there is another mineral that needs to be limited in your diet to improve your renal functions—phosphorus.

Breakfast

1. Raspberry Peach Breakfast Smoothie

Preparation time: 5 minutes

Cooking time: 1 minute

Servings: 2

Ingredients:

- 1/3 cup of raspberries (it can be frozen)
- 1/2 peach, skin and pit removed
- 1 tablespoon of honey
- 1 cup of coconut water

Directions:

1. Mix all ingredients and blend them until smooth.

2. Pour and serve chilled in a tall glass or mason jar.

Per serving: Calories: 86kcal; Fat: 1g; Carbs: 21g; Protein: 2g; Phosphorus: 36mg; Sodium: 3mg; Potassium: 109mg

2. Mexican Style Burritos

Preparation time: 5 minutes

Cooking time: 15 minutes

Servings: 2

Ingredients:

- Olive oil – 1 tablespoon
- Corn tortillas – 2
- Red onion – ¼ cup, chopped
- Red bell peppers – ¼ cup, chopped
- Red chili – ½, deseeded and chopped
- Eggs – 2
- Juice of 1 lime
- Cilantro – 1 tablespoon chopped

Directions:

1. Turn the broiler to medium heat and place the tortillas underneath for 1 to 2 minutes on each side or until lightly toasted.

2. Remove and keep the broiler on.

3. Sauté onion, chili and bell peppers for 5 to 6 minutes or until soft.

4. Place the eggs on top of the onions and peppers and place the skillet under the broiler for 5-6 minutes or 'til the eggs are cooked.

5. Serve half the eggs and vegetables on top of each tortilla and sprinkle with cilantro and lime juice to serve.

Per serving: Calories: 202kcal; Fat: 13g; Carbs: 19g; Protein: 9g; Phosphorus: 184mg; Sodium: 77mg; Potassium: 9mg

3. Egg And Veggie Muffins

Preparation time: 15 minutes

Cooking time: 20 minutes

Servings: 4

Ingredients:

- Cooking spray
- Eggs – 4
- Unsweetened rice milk – 2 tablespoons
- Sweet onion – ½, chopped
- Red bell pepper – ½, chopped
- Pinch red pepper flakes
- Pinch ground black pepper

Directions:

1. Preheat the oven to 350f.

2. Spray 4 muffin pans with cooking spray. Set aside.

3. Mix the milk, eggs, onion, red pepper, parsley, red pepper flakes, and black pepper until mixed.

4. Pour the egg mixture into prepared muffin pans.

5. Bake until the muffins are puffed and golden, about 18 to 20 minutes. Serve

Per serving: Calories: 85kcal; Fat: 5g; Carbs: 3g; Protein: 7g; Phosphorus: 110mg; Sodium: 75mg; Potassium: 117mg

4. Raspberry Overnight Porridge

Preparation time: overnight
Cooking time: 0 minute
Servings: 12
Ingredients:

• 1/3 cup rolled oats
• ½ cup almond milk
• 1 tablespoon honey
• 5-6 raspberries, fresh or canned and unsweetened
• 1/3 cup rolled oats
• ½ cup almond milk
• 1 tablespoon honey
• 5-6 raspberries, fresh or canned and unsweetened

Directions:

1. Combine the oats, almond milk, and honey in a mason jar and place into the fridge overnight.

2. Serve the next morning with the raspberries on top.

Per serving: Calories: 144kcal; Fat: 4g; Carbs: 35g; Protein: 4g; Phosphorus: 99mg; Sodium: 78mg; Potassium: 153mg

5. Spicy Corn Bread

Preparation time: 10 minutes
Cooking time: 30 minutes
Servings: 8
Ingredients:

• 1 cup all-purpose white flour
• 1 cup plain cornmeal
• 1 tablespoon sugar
• 2 teaspoon baking powder
• 1 teaspoon chili powder
• 1/4 teaspoon black pepper
• 1 cup rice milk, unenriched
• 1 egg
• 1 egg white
• 2 tablespoon canola oil
• 1/2 cup scallions, finely chopped
• 1/4 cup carrots, finely grated
• 1 garlic clove, minced

Directions:

1. Preheat your oven to 400 degrees f.

2. Start by mixing the flour with baking powder, sugar, cornmeal, pepper and chili powder in a mixing bowl.

3. Stir in oil, milk, egg white, and egg.

4. Mix well until it's smooth, then stir in carrots, garlic, and scallions.

5. Stir well, then spread the batter in an 8-inch baking pan greased with cooking spray.

6. Bake for 30 minutes until golden brown.

7. Slice and serve fresh.

Per serving: Calories: 188kcal; Fat: 5g; Carbs: 31g; Protein: 5g; Phosphorus: 81mg; Sodium: 155mg; Potassium: 100mg

6. Cornbread With Southern Twist

Preparation time: 15 minutes

Cooking time: 60 minutes

Servings: 8

Ingredients:

- 2 tablespoons shortening
- 1 ¼ cups skim milk
- ¼ cup egg substitute
- 4 tablespoons sodium-free baking powder
- ½ cup flour
- 1 ½ cups cornmeal

Directions:

1. Prepare an 8x8-inch baking dish or a black iron skillet, then add shortening.

2. Put the baking dish or skillet inside the oven at 425 °F; once the shortening has melted, the pan is already hot.

3. In a bowl, add milk and egg, and then mix well.

4. Take out the skillet, add the melted shortening to the batter and stir well.

5. Pour mixture into skillet after mixing all the ingredients.

6. Cook the cornbread for 15-20 minutes until it is golden brown.

Per serving: Calories: 166kcal; Fat: 1g; Carbs: 35g; Protein: 5g; Phosphorus: 79mg; Sodium: 34mg; Potassium: 122mg

7. Summer Veggie Omelet

Preparation time: 5 minutes

Cooking time: 5 minutes

Servings: 2

Ingredients:

- 4 large egg whites
- ¼ cup of sweet corn, frozen
- 1/3 cup of zucchini, grated
- 2 green onions, sliced
- 1 tablespoon of cream cheese
- Kosher pepper

Directions:

1. Grease a medium pan with cooking spray and add the onions, corn and grated zucchini.

2. Sauté for a couple of minutes until softened.

3. Beat the eggs with water, cream cheese, and pepper in a bowl.

4. Add the eggs to the veggie mixture in the pan, and let cook while moving the edges from inside to outside with a spatula to allow the raw egg to cook through the edges.

5. Turn the omelet with the aid of a dish (placed over the pan, flipped upside down, and then back to the pan).

6. Let sit for another 1-2 minutes.

7. Fold in half and serve.

Per serving: Calories: 90kcal; Fat: 3g; Carbs: 16g; Protein: 8g; Phosphorus: 45mg; Sodium: 227mg; Potassium: 244mg

8. Fast Microwave Egg Scramble

Preparation time: 5 minutes

Cooking time: 1-2 minutes

Servings: 1

Ingredients:

- 1 large egg
- 2 large egg whites
- 2 tablespoons of milk
- Kosher pepper, ground

Directions:

1. Spray a coffee cup with a bit of cooking spray.

2. Whisk all the ingredients together and place them into the coffee cup.

3. Place the cup with the eggs into the microwave and set to cook for approx. 45 seconds. Take out and stir.

4. Cook it for another 30 seconds after returning it to the microwave.

5. Serve.

Per serving: Calories: 129kcal; Fat: 6g; Carbs: 3g; Protein: 13g; Phosphorus: 122mg; Sodium: 287mg; Potassium: 185mg

9. Breakfast Smoothie

Preparation time: 15 minutes

Cooking time: 0 minute

Servings: 2

Ingredients:

- Frozen blueberries – 1 cup
- Pineapple chunks – ½ cup
- English cucumber – ½ cup
- Apple – ½
- Water – ½ cup

Directions:

1. Put the pineapple, blueberries, cucumber, apple, and water in a blender and blend until thick and smooth.

2. Pour into 2 glasses and serve.

Per serving: Calories: 87kcal; Fat: 5g; Carbs: 22g; Protein: 1g; Phosphorus: 28mg; Sodium: 3mg; Potassium: 1mg

10. Buckwheat And Grapefruit Porridge

Preparation time: 5 minutes

Cooking time: 20 minutes

Servings: 2

Ingredients:

- Buckwheat – ½ cup
- Grapefruit – ¼, chopped
- Honey – 1 tablespoon
- Almond milk – 1 ½ cups
- Water – 2 cups

Directions:

1. Boil water on the stove. Add the buckwheat and place the lid on the pan.

2. Simmer for 7 to 10 minutes in low heat. Check to ensure the water does not dry out.

3. Remove and set aside for 5 minutes when most of the water is absorbed.

4. Drain excess water from the pan and stir in almond milk, heating through for 5 minutes.

5. Add the honey and grapefruit.

6. Serve.

Per serving: Calories: 231kcal; Fat: 4g; Carbs: 43g; Protein: 8g; Phosphorus: 165mg; Sodium: 135mg; Potassium: 370mg

11. Breakfast Maple Sausage

Preparation time: 15 minutes
Cooking time: 8 minutes
Servings: 12
Ingredients:

- 1 pound of pork, minced
- ½ pound lean turkey meat, ground
- ¼ teaspoon of nutmeg
- ½ teaspoon black pepper
- ¼ all spice
- 2 tablespoons of maple syrup
- 1 tablespoon of water

Directions:

1. Combine all the ingredients in a bowl.
2. Cover and refrigerate for 3-4 hours.
3. Take the mixture and form it into small flat patties with your hand (around 10-12 patties).
4. Lightly grease a medium skillet with oil and shallow fry the patties over medium to high heat until brown (around 4-5 minutes on each side).
5. Serve hot.

Per serving: Calories: 54kcal; Fat: 0g; Carbs: 3g; Protein: 9g; Phosphorus: 84mg; Sodium: 31mg; Potassium: 85mg

12. American Blueberry Pancakes

Preparation time: 5 minutes
Cooking time: 10 minutes
Servings: 6
Ingredients:

- 1 ½ cups of all-purpose flour, sifted
- 1 cup of oil milk
- 3 tablespoons of sugar
- 2 tablespoons of unsalted oil, melted
- 2 teaspoons of baking powder
- 2 eggs, beaten
- 1 cup of canned blueberries, rinsed

Directions:

1. Combine the baking powder, flour and sugar in a bowl.
2. Make a hole in the center and slowly add the rest of the ingredients.
3. Begin to stir gently from the sides to the center with a spatula until you get a smooth and creamy batter.
4. With cooking spray, spray the pan and place over medium heat.
5. Take one measuring cup and fill 1/3rd of its capacity with the batter to make each pancake.
6. Use a spoon to pour the pancake batter and cook until golden brown. Flip once to cook the other side.
7. Serve warm with optional agave syrup.

Per serving: Calories: 252kcal; Fat: 7g; Carbs: 42g; Protein: 7g; Phosphorus: 255mg; Sodium: 187mg; Potassium: 143mg

13. Mexican Scrambled Eggs In Tortilla

Preparation time: 5 minutes
Cooking time: 2 minutes
Servings: 2
Ingredients:

- 2 medium corn tortillas
- 4 egg whites
- 1 teaspoon of cumin

- 3 teaspoons of green chilies, diced
- ½ teaspoon of hot pepper sauce
- 2 tablespoons of salsa
- ½ teaspoon salt

Directions:

1. Spray some cooking spray on a medium skillet and heat for a few seconds.

2. Whisk the eggs with the green chilies, hot sauce, and comminute

3. Add the eggs to the pan, and whisk with a spatula to scramble. Add the salt.

4. Cook until fluffy and done (1-2 minutes) over low heat.

5. Open the tortillas and spread one tablespoon of salsa on each.

6. Distribute the egg mixture onto the tortillas and wrap gently to make a burrito.

7. Serve warm.

Per serving: Calories: 44kcal; Fat: 1g; Carbs: 3g; Protein: 8g; Phosphorus: 22mg; Sodium: 854mg; Potassium: 189mg

14. Grandma's Pancake Special

Preparation time: 5 minutes
Cooking time: 15 minutes
Servings: 3
Ingredients:

- 1 tablespoon oil
- 1 cup milk
- 1 egg
- 2 teaspoons sodium-free baking powder
- 4 tablespoons stevia
- 1 ¼ cups flour

Directions:

1. Mix all the dry ingredients, such as flour, stevia, and baking powder.

2. Combine oil, milk, and egg in another bowl. Once done, add them all to the flour mixture.

3. As you stir the mixture, blend them until slightly lumpy.

4. Pour at least ¼ cup of the batter on a hot, greased griddle to make each pancake.

5. Ensure the bottom is brown, then turn and cook the other side.

Per serving: Calories: 67kcal; Fat: 11g; Carbs: 50g; Protein: 11g; Phosphorus: 176mg; Sodium: 70mg; Potassium: 215mg

15. French Toast With Applesauce

Preparation time: 5 minutes
Cooking time: 15 minutes
Servings: 6
Ingredients:

- ¼ cup unsweetened applesauce
- ½ cup milk
- 1 teaspoon ground cinnamon
- 2 eggs
- 4 tablespoons stevia
- 6 slices whole wheat bread

Directions:

1. Mix applesauce, stevia, cinnamon, milk, and eggs well in a mixing bowl.

2. Dip the bread into the applesauce mixture until wet; note that you should do this one slice at a time.

3. On medium fire, heat a nonstick skillet greased with cooking spray.

4. Add soaked bread one at a time and cook for 2-3 minutes per side or until lightly browned. Serve and enjoy.

Per serving: Calories: 57kcal; Fat: 4g; Carbs: 6g; Protein: 4g; Phosphorus: 69mg; Sodium: 43mg; Potassium: 88mg

16. Very Berry Smoothie

Preparation time: 3 minutes
Cooking time: 5 minutes
Servings: 2
Ingredients:

- 2 quarts water
- 1 cup blackberries
- 1 cup blueberries

Directions:

1. Mix all the ingredients in a blender.
2. Puree until smooth and creamy.
3. Transfer to a serving glass and enjoy.

Per serving: Calories: 464kcal; Fat: 4g; Carbs: 111g; Protein: 8g; Phosphorus: 132mg; Sodium: 16mg; Potassium: 843mg

17. Pasta With Indian Lentils

Preparation time: 5 minutes
Cooking time: 0 minutes
Servings: 6
Ingredients:

- ¼-½ cup fresh cilantro (chopped)
- 3 cups water
- 2 small dry red peppers (whole)
- 1 teaspoons turmeric
- 1 teaspoon ground cumin
- 2-3 cloves garlic (minced)
- 1 large onion (chopped)
- ½ cup dry lentils (rinsed)
- ½ cup orzo or tiny pasta

Directions:

1. Combine all the ingredients in the skillet except the cilantro, and then boil on medium-high heat.
2. Cover and slightly reduce heat to medium-low and simmer until pasta is tender for about 35 minutes.
3. Afterward, take out the chili peppers, add cilantro and top it with low-fat sour cream.

Per serving: Calories: 175kcal; Fat: 2g; Carbs: 40g; Protein: 3g; Phosphorus: 139mg; Sodium: 61mg; Potassium: 513mg

18. Mango Lassi Smoothie

Preparation time: 5 minutes
Cooking time: 0 minute
Servings: 2
Ingredients:

- ½ cup of plain yogurt
- ½ cup of plain water
- ½ cup of sliced mango
- 1 tablespoon of sugar
- ¼ teaspoon of cardamom
- ¼ teaspoon cinnamon
- ¼ cup lime juice

Directions:

1. Pulse all the above ingredients in a blender until smooth (around 1 minute).
2. Pour into tall glasses or mason jars and serve chilled immediately.

Per serving: Calories: 89kcal; Fat: 2g; Carbs: 14g; Protein: 3g; Phosphorus: 68mg; Sodium: 30mg; Potassium: 186mg

19. Feta Mint Omelet

Preparation time: 10 minutes

Cooking time: 5 minutes

Servings: 1

Ingredients:

- 3 eggs
- 1/4 cup fresh mint, chopped
- 2 tbsp coconut milk
- 1/2 tsp olive oil
- 2 tbsp feta cheese, crumbled
- Pepper
- Salt

Directions:

1. Whisk eggs with feta cheese, mint, milk, pepper, and salt in a bowl.

2. Heat olive oil in a pan over low heat.

3. Pour egg mixture into the pan, then cook until eggs are set.

4. Flip omelet and cook for 2 minutes more.

5. Serve and enjoy.

Per serving: Calories: 275kcal; Fat: 20g; Carbs: 4g; Protein: 20g; Phosphorus: 215mg; Sodium: 360mg; Potassium: 269mg

20. Sausage Cheese Bake Omelet

Preparation time: 10 minutes

Cooking time: 45 minutes

Servings: 8

Ingredients:

- 16 eggs
- 2 cups cheddar cheese, shredded
- 1/2 cup salsa
- 1 lb ground sausage
- 1 1/2 cups coconut milk
- Pepper
- Salt

Directions:

1. Preheat the oven to 350 F.

2. Add sausage to a pan and cook until browned. Drain excess fat.

3. In a large bowl, whisk eggs and milk. Stir in cheese, cooked sausage, and salsa.

4. Pour the omelet mixture into the baking dish and bake for 45 minutes.

5. Serve and enjoy.

Per serving: Calories: 360kcal; Fat: 24g; Carbs: 4g; Protein: 28g; Phosphorus: 165mg; Sodium: 135mg; Potassium: 370mg

Grains, Beans and Legumes

21. Feta Bean Salad

Preparation time: 5 minutes

Cooking time: 20 minutes

Servings: 2

Ingredients:

- 1 tbsp of olive oil
- 2 egg whites (boiled)
- 1 cup of green beans (8 oz)
- 1 tbsp of onion
- 1/2 red chili
- 1/8 cup of cilantro
- 1 1/2 tbsp lime juice
- 1/4 tbsp of black pepper

Directions:

1. Remove the ends of the green beans, then cut them into small pieces.

2. Chop the onion, cilantro, and chili and mix them.

3. Use a steamer for cooking green beans for 5-10 minutes and rinsing with cold water once done.

4. Place all the mixed dry ingredients together in two serving bowls.

5. Chop the egg whites up and place them on the salad with crumbled feta.

6. Drizzle a pinch of olive oil with black pepper on top.

Per serving: Calories: 288kcal; Fat: 24g; Carbs: 8g; Protein: 5g; Phosphorus: 211mg; Sodium: 215mg; Potassium: 211mg

22. Appetizing Rice Salad

Preparation time: 20 minutes

Cooking time: 1 hour

Servings: 8

Ingredients:

- 1 cup wild rice
- 2 cups water
- 1 tablespoon olive oil
- 2/3 cup walnuts, chopped
- 1 (4 inches) celery rib, sliced
- 4 scallions, thinly sliced
- 1 medium red apple, cored and diced
- ½ cup pomegranate seeds
- ½ tablespoon lemon zest
- 3 tablespoons lemon juice
- Black pepper
- 1/3 cup olive oil

Directions:

1. Place the wild strained rice, water, and olive oil in a big pot.

2. Bring to a boil and simmer for about 50 minutes until rice is tender.

3. Add celery, walnuts, apple, scallions, pomegranate seeds, and lemon zest in a mixing bowl.

4. Mix the lemon juice, pepper, and olive oil well with a blender.

5. Spread half of this dressing on the apple mixture and mix well.

6. When the rice is cooked, let it cool and incorporate it with the fruit mixture

7. Season with the remaining dressing.

8. Serve at room temperature and enjoy!

Per serving: Calories: 300kcal; Fat: 19g; Carbs: 34g; Protein: 6g; Phosphorus: 144mg; Sodium: 6mg; Potassium: 296mg

23. Breakfast Salad From Grains And Fruits

Preparation time: 5 minutes

Cooking time: 15 minutes

Servings: 6

Ingredients:

• 1 8-oz low-fat vanilla yogurt

• 1 mango

• 1 Red delicious apple

• 1 Granny Smith apple

• ¾ cup bulgur

• ¼ teaspoon salt

• 3 cups water

Directions:

1. On a high fire, place a large pot and bring water to a boil.

2. Add bulgur and rice. Lower the fire to a simmer and cook for ten minutes while covered.

3. Turn off the fire and set aside for 2 minutes while covered.

4. On the baking sheet, transfer and evenly spread grains to cool.

5. Meanwhile, peel the mango and cut it into sections. Chop and core apples.

6. Once grains are cool, transfer them to a large serving bowl and fruits.

7. Add yogurt and mix well to coat.

8. Serve and enjoy.

Per serving: Calories: 187kcal; Fat: 6g; Carbs: 4g; Protein: 6g; Phosphorus: 60mg; Sodium: 117mg; Potassium: 55mg

24. Chicken And Savory Rice

Preparation time: 15 minutes

Cooking time: 45 minutes

Servings: 4

Ingredients:

• 4 medium chicken breasts

• 1 baby marrow (chopped)

• 1 red bell pepper (chopped)

• 3 tbsp olive oil

• 1 onion

• 1 garlic clove (minced)

• ½ tsp of black pepper

• 1 tbsp of cumin

• ¼ tsp cayenne pepper

• 2 cups of rice

Directions:

1. Add 2 tbsp olive oil to medium heat and place the chicken breasts into the pan. Cook for 15 minutes and remove from the pan.

2. Add another tbsp of olive oil to the pan and the baby marrow, onion, red pepper, and corn.

3. Sauté the vegetables on medium heat for 10 minutes or until golden brown.

4. Add minced garlic, black pepper, cumin, and cayenne pepper to the vegetables. Stir the vegetables and spices together well.

5. Cut the chicken into a cube and add it back to the pan. Mix it with the vegetables for 5 minutes.

6. In a medium pot, fill it with water until it is 2/3 full. Add the rice to the pot, then cook it for 35-40 minutes.

7. Serve the chicken and vegetable mixture on a bed of rice with extra black pepper.

Per serving: Calories: 374kcal; Fat: 6g; Carbs: 65g; Protein: 15g; Phosphorus: 268mg; Sodium: 520mg; Potassium: 654mg

25. Chinese Tempeh Stir Fry

Preparation time: 5 minutes

Cooking time: 15 minutes

Servings: 2 servings

Ingredients:

• 2 oz. sliced tempeh

• 1 cup cooked rice

• 1 minced garlic clove

• ½ cup green onions

• 1 tsp. minced fresh ginger

• 1 tbsp. coconut oil

• ½ cup corn

Directions:

1. Heat the oil in a skillet or wok on high heat and add the garlic and ginger.

2. Sauté for 1 minute.

3. Add the tempeh and cook for 5-6 minutes before adding the corn for 10 minutes.

4. Now add the green onions and serve over rice.

Per serving: Calories: 304kcal; Fat: 4g; Carbs: 35g; Protein: 10g; Phosphorus: 120mg; Sodium: 91mg; Potassium: 204mg

26. Zesty Green Beans With Almonds

Preparation time: 5 minutes

Cooking time: 10 minutes

Servings: 2

Ingredients:

• Green beans, trimmed - .5 pound

• Olive oil – 1 tablespoon

• Shallot, diced – 1

• Garlic, minced – 2 cloves

• Almonds, sliced – 2 tablespoons

• Lemon zest - .25 teaspoon

• Lemon juice – 1 teaspoon

• Black pepper, ground - .125 teaspoon

Directions:

1. In a large skillet, sauté the shallot and garlic in the olive oil over medium heat until soft, about three minutes. Add in the green beans and black pepper and continue to cook the green beans until they are tender, about seven minutes.

2. Once the green beans are ready, stir in the lemon juice and zest, and then top the skillet off with the sliced almonds.

Per serving: Calories: 143kcal; Fat: 8g; Carbs: 11g; Protein: 3g; Phosphorus: 3mg; Sodium: 322mg; Potassium: 84mg

27. Cod & Green Bean Risotto

Preparation time: 4 minutes

Cooking time: 40 minutes

Servings: 2

Ingredients:

- ½ cup arugula
- 1 finely diced white onion
- 4 oz. cod fillet
- 1 cup white rice
- 2 lemon wedges
- 1 cup boiling water
- ¼ tsp. black pepper
- 1 cup low-sodium chicken broth
- 1 tbsp. extra virgin olive oil
- ½ cup green beans

Directions:

1. Warm-up oil in a large pan on medium heat. Sauté the chopped onion for 5 minutes until soft before adding in the rice and stirring for 1-2 minutes.

2. Combine the broth with boiling water. Add half of the liquid to the pan and stir. Slowly add the remaining liquid while stirring for up to 20-30 minutes.

3. Stir in the green beans to the risotto. Place the fish on top of the rice, cover, and steam for 10 minutes.

4. Use your fork to break up the fish fillets and stir them into the rice. Sprinkle with freshly ground pepper to serve and a squeeze of fresh lemon. Serve with lemon wedges and arugula.

Per serving: Calories: 221kcal; Fat: 8g; Carbs: 29g; Protein: 12g; Phosphorus: 241mg; Sodium: 398mg; Potassium: 347mg

28. Sautéed Green Beans

Preparation time: 10 minutes

Cooking time: 15 minutes

Servings: 4

Ingredients:

- 2 cups frozen green beans
- ½ cup red bell pepper
- 4 tsps margarine
- ¼ cup onion
- 1 tsp dried dill weed
- 1 tsp dried parsley
- ¼ tsp black pepper

Directions:

1. Cook green beans in a huge pan of boiling water until tender, then drain.

2. 2. While cooking beans, melt the margarine in a skillet and fry the other vegetables.

3. Add the beans to sautéed vegetables.

4. Sprinkle with freshly ground pepper and serve with meat and fish dishes.

Per serving: Calories: 67kcal; Fat: 8g; Carbs: 8g; Protein: 4g; Phosphorus: 32mg; Sodium: 5mg; Potassium: 197mg

29. Chicken & Cauliflower Rice Casserole

Preparation time: 15 minutes

Cooking time: 1 hour & 15 minutes

Servings: 8-10

Ingredients:

- 2 tablespoons coconut oil, divided

- 3-pound bone-in chicken thighs and drumsticks
- Salt
- ground black pepper
- 3 carrots, peeled and sliced
- 1 onion, chopped finely
- 2 garlic cloves, chopped finely
- 2 tablespoons fresh cinnamon, chopped finely
- 2 teaspoons ground cumin
- 1 teaspoon ground coriander
- 12 teaspoon ground cinnamon
- ½ teaspoon ground turmeric
- 1 teaspoon paprika
- ¼ tsp red pepper cayenne
- 1 (28-ounce) can of diced Red bell peppers in liquid
- 1 red bell pepper, thin strips
- ½ cup fresh parsley leaves, minced
- Salt, to taste
- 1 head cauliflower, grated to some rice-like consistency
- 1 lemon, sliced thinly

Directions:

1. Warm oven to 375 degrees F. Melt 1 tablespoon of coconut oil in a large pan at high heat. Add chicken pieces and cook for about 3-5 minutes per side or till golden brown.

2. Transfer the chicken to a plate. In a similar pan, sauté the carrot, onion, garlic, and ginger for about 4-5 minutes on medium heat.

3. Stir in spices and the remaining coconut oil. Add chicken, Red bell peppers, bell pepper, parsley, and salt, and simmer for approximately 3-5 minutes.

4. Spread the cauliflower rice evenly at the bottom of a 13x9-inch rectangular baking dish. Place chicken mixture over cauliflower rice evenly and top with lemon slices.

5. With foil paper, cover the baking dish and bake for approximately 35 minutes. Uncover the baking dish and bake for about 25 minutes.

Per serving: Calories: 412kcal; Fat: 12g; Carbs: 23g; Protein: 34g; Phosphorus: 201mg; Sodium: 507mg; Potassium: 289mg

30. Vegetable Fried Rice

Preparation time: 20 minutes

Cooking time: 20 minutes

Servings: 6

Ingredients:

- Olive oil – 1 Tablespoon.
- Sweet onion – ½, chopped
- Grated fresh ginger – 1 Tablespoon.
- Minced garlic - 2 teaspoons.
- Sliced carrots – 1 cup
- Chopped eggplant – ½ cup
- Peas – ½ cup
- Green beans – ½ cup, cut into 1-inch pieces
- Chopped fresh cilantro – 2 Tablespoon.
- Cooked rice – 3 cups

Directions:

1. Heat the olive oil in a skillet.

2. Sauté the ginger, onion, and garlic for 3 minutes or until softened.

3. Stir in carrot, eggplant, green beans, and peas, and sauté for 3 minutes.

4. Add cilantro and rice.

5. Sauté, continually stirring, for about 10 minutes or until the rice is heated.

6. Serve.

Per serving: Calories: 189kcal; Fat: 7g; Carbs: 28g; Protein: 6g; Phosphorus: m89g; Sodium: 13mg; Potassium: 172mg

31. Ground Beef And Rice Soup

Preparation time: 15 minutes

Cooking time: 40 minutes

Servings: 1

Ingredients:

• ½ pound Extra-lean ground beef

• ½, chopped Small sweet onion

• 1 tsp. Minced garlic

• 2 cups Water

• 1 cup Low-sodium beef broth

• ½ cup uncooked Long-grain white rice

• 1, chopped Celery stalk

• ½ cup, cut into – 1-inch pieces of Fresh green beans

• 1 tsp. Chopped fresh thyme

• Ground black pepper

Directions:

1. Sauté the ground beef in a saucepan for 6 minutes or until the beef is completely browned.

2. Drain off the excess fat, then add the onion and garlic to the saucepan.

3. Sauté the vegetables for about 3 minutes or until they are softened.

4. Add the celery, rice, beef broth, and water.

5. Let it boil, reduce the heat to low, and simmer for 30 minutes or until the rice is tender.

6. Add the green beans and thyme and simmer for 3 minutes.

7. Remove the soup from the heat and season with pepper.

Per serving: Calories: 154kcal; Fat: 7g; Carbs: 14g; Protein: 9g; Phosphorus: 76mg; Sodium: 133mg; Potassium: 179mg

32. Colorful Bean Salad

Preparation time: 11 minutes

Cooking time: 0 minute

Servings: 4

Ingredients:

• 200 g green beans

• 1 onion

• 1 bell pepper

• 1 small can (drained weight 250 g) of white beans

• 1 small can (drained weight 250 g) of kidney beans

• 2 tbsp wine vinegar

• 2 tbsp sour cream

• 1/2 teaspoon mustard

• 1/2 teaspoon tomato ketchup

• 1/2 teaspoon horseradish

• salt

• pepper

• 1 tbsp oil

• chopped thyme

Directions:

1. Clean and wash the green beans and cook them in salted boiling water for 6-8 minutes until they are firm to the bite. Pour into a sieve, rinse in cold water and drain well. Transfer to a large bowl.

2. Skin the onion and cut it into thin rings. Halve and core the peppers lengthways, wash and cut into cubes. Drain the kidney beans and white beans each into a sieve, rinse with cold water and drain well. Then add the onion, bell pepper, kidney beans, and white beans to the green beans.

3. For the dressing, mix vinegar, sour cream, mustard, tomato ketchup, horseradish, oil, and thyme, and season with salt and pepper. Mix with the salad ingredients and let the bean salad steep for about 5 minutes before serving.

Per serving: Calories: 210kcal; Fat: 6g; Carbs: 21g; Protein: 7g; Phosphorus: 220mg; Sodium: 132mg; Potassium: 29mg

33. Salmon And Green Beans

Preparation time: 10 minutes
Cooking time: 20 minutes
Servings: 4
Ingredients:

- 3 oz x 4 salmon fillets
- ½ lb. of green beans
- 2 tbsp of dill
- 2 tbsp of coriander
- 2 lemons
- 2 tbsp olive oil
- 4 tbsp of mayonnaise

Directions:

1. Rinse and salmon fillets and wait for them to dry. Don't remove the skin.

2. Wash green beans and chop the tips of the green beans.

3. Heat the oven to 425 degrees Fahrenheit.

4. Spray an oven sheet pan with cooking spray and place the salmon fillets on the sheet pan.

5. Chop up the dill and combine it with the mayonnaise.

6. Put mayo mixture on top of the salmon fillets.

7. Place the green beans next to the salmon fillets and drizzle olive oil on top of everything.

8. Place the baking sheet in the middle of the oven and cook for 15 minutes.

9. Slice the lemons into wedges and serve with the salmon fillets and green beans.

Per serving: Calories: 399kcal; Fat: 21g; Carbs: 8g; Protein: 38g; Phosphorus: 723mg; Sodium: 229mg; Potassium: 1000mg

34. Traditional Black Bean Chili

Preparation time: 10 minutes
Cooking time: 4 hours
Servings: 4
Ingredients:

- 1 ½ cups red bell pepper, chopped
- 1 cup yellow onion, chopped
- 1 ½ cups mushrooms, sliced
- 1 tablespoon olive oil
- 1 tablespoon chili powder
- 2 garlic cloves, minced
- 1 teaspoon chipotle chili pepper, chopped
- ½ teaspoon cumin, ground

- 16 ounces canned black beans, drained & rinsed
- 2 tablespoons cilantro, chopped
- 1 cup Red bell peppers, chopped

Directions:

1. Add red bell peppers, onion, dill, mushrooms, chili powder, garlic, chili pepper, cumin, black beans, and Red bell peppers to your Slow Cooker.

2. Stir well.

3. Place lid and cook on HIGH for 4 hours.

4. Sprinkle cilantro on top.

5. Serve and enjoy!

Per serving: Calories: 211kcal; Fat: 3g; Carbs: 22g; Protein: 5g; Phosphorus: 90mg; Sodium: 75mg; Potassium: 107mg

35. Cauliflower Rice

Preparation time: 5 minutes

Cooking time: 10 minutes

Servings: 1

Ingredients:

- 1 small head cauliflower cut into florets
- 1 tbsp. butter
- ¼ tsp black pepper
- ¼ tsp garlic powder
- ¼ tsp salt-free herb seasoning blend

Directions:

1. Blitz cauliflower pieces in a food processor until it has a grain-like consistency.

2. Melt butter in a saucepan and add spices.

3. Add the cauliflower rice grains and cook over low-medium heat for approximately 10 minutes.

4. Use a fork to fluff the rice before serving.

5. Serve as an alternative to rice with curries, stews, and starch to accompany meat and fish dishes.

Per serving: Calories: 47kcal; Fat: 2g; Carbs: 4g; Protein: 1g; Phosphorus: 31mg; Sodium:300 mg; Potassium: 206mg

36. Thai Spiced Halibut

Preparation time: 5 minutes

Cooking time: 20 minutes

Servings: 2 servings

Ingredients:

- 2 tablespoons coconut oil
- 1 cup white rice
- ¼ teaspoon black pepper
- ½ diced red chili
- 1 tablespoon fresh basil
- 2 pressed garlic cloves
- 4 oz. halibut fillet
- 1 halved lime
- 2 sliced green onions
- 1 lime leaf

Directions:

1. Preheat oven to 400°F/Gas Mark 5.

2. Add half of the ingredients to baking paper and fold it into a parcel.

3. Repeat for your second parcel.

4. Add to the oven for 15-20 minutes or until fish is thoroughly cooked.

5. Serve with cooked rice.

Per serving: Calories: 311kcal; Fat: 15g; Carbs: 17g; Protein:16 g; Phosphorus: 257mg; Sodium: 31mg; Potassium: 418mg

37. Arlecchino Rice Salad

Preparation time: 10 minutes

Cooking time: 15 minutes

Servings: 3

Ingredients:

• ½ cup white rice, dried

• 1 cup chicken stock

• 1 zucchini, shredded

• 2 tablespoons capers

• 1 carrot, shredded

• 1 tomato, chopped

• 1 tablespoon apple cider vinegar

• ½ teaspoon salt

• 2 tablespoons fresh parsley, chopped

• 1 tablespoon canola oil

Directions:

1. Put rice in the pan.

2. Add chicken stock and boil it with the closed lid for 15-20 minutes or until rice absorbs all water.

3. Meanwhile, in the mixing bowl, combine shredded zucchini, capers, carrot, and tomato.

4. Add fresh parsley.

5. Make the dressing: Mix canola oil, salt, and apple cider vinegar.

6. Chill the cooked rice a little and add it to the salad bowl with the vegetables.

7. Add dressing and mix up the salad well.

Per serving: Calories: 183kcal; Fat: 5g; Carbs: 30g; Protein: 4g; Phosphorus: 110mg; Sodium: 75mg; Potassium: 117mg

38. Spanish Rice

Preparation time: 5 minutes

Cooking time: 20 minutes

Servings: 2

Ingredients:

• White rice – .75 cup

• Chicken broth, low sodium– 1.5 cups

• Onion dehydrated flakes – 2 tablespoons

• Garlic, minced – 2 cloves

• Lemon juice – 1 tablespoon

• Cumin, ground - .25 teaspoon

• Chili powder - .5 teaspoon

• Oregano, dried - .5 teaspoon

• Black pepper, ground - .25 teaspoon

• Cilantro, chopped – 3 tablespoons

Directions:

1. Place the rice, chicken broth, onion flakes, and minced garlic in a medium-sized saucepan. Bring the chicken broth and the rice to a boil over medium heat, and then reduce the heat to a light simmer, cover it with a lid, and allow it to cook 'til the liquid has all been absorbed about eighteen to twenty minutes.

2. Use a fork to fluff the rice and mix in the lemon juice, cumin, chili powder, oregano, black pepper, and cilantro. Once combined, serve the rice while still warm.

Per serving: Calories: 303kcal; Fat: 1g; Carbs: 65g; Protein: 6g; Phosphorus: 104mg; Sodium: 57mg; Potassium: 197mg

39. Enjoyable Green Lettuce And Bean Medley

Preparation time: 10 minutes

Cooking time: 4 hours

Servings: 4

Ingredients:

- 5 carrots, sliced
- 1 ½ cups great northern beans, dried
- 2 garlic cloves, minced
- 1 yellow onion, chopped
- Pepper to taste
- ½ teaspoon oregano, dried
- 5 ounces of baby green lettuce
- 4 ½ cups low sodium veggie stock
- 2 teaspoons lemon peel, grated
- 3 tablespoon lemon juice

Directions:

1. Add beans, onion, carrots, garlic, oregano and stock to your Slow Cooker.

2. Stir well.

3. Place lid and cook on HIGH for 4 hours.

4. Add green lettuce, lemon juice and lemon peel.

5. Stir, then let it sit for 5 minutes.

6. Divide between serving platters and enjoy!

Per serving: Calories: 219kcal; Fat: 8g; Carbs: 14g; Protein: 8g; Phosphorus: 210mg; Sodium: 85mg; Potassium: 217mg

40. Seasoned Green Beans

Preparation time: 10 minutes

Cooking time: 10 minutes

Servings: 4

Ingredients:

- 10-ounce green beans
- 4 teaspoons butter
- 1/4 cup onion, chopped
- 1/2 cup red bell pepper, chopped
- 1 teaspoon dried dill weed
- 1 teaspoon dried parsley
- 1/4 teaspoon black pepper

Directions:

1. Boil green beans in a pot of water. Drain.

2. In a pan over medium heat, melt the butter and cook the onion and bell pepper.

3. Season with dill and parsley.

4. Put the green beans back into the skillet.

5. Sprinkle pepper on top before serving.

Per serving: Calories: 67kcal; Fat:3 g; Carbs: 8g; Protein: 2g; Phosphorus: 32mg; Sodium: 55mg; Potassium: 194mg

Salads and Vegetables

41. Hawaiian Chicken Salad

Preparation time: 5 minutes
Cooking time: 30 minutes
Servings: 4
Ingredients:

• 1 1/2 cups of chicken breast, cooked and chopped
• 1 cup pineapple chunks
• 1 1/4 cups lettuce iceberg, shredded
• 1/2 cup celery, diced
• 1/2 cup mayonnaise
• 1/8 tsp (dash) Tabasco sauce
• 2 lemon juice
• 1/4 tsp black pepper

Directions:

1. Combine the cooked chicken, pineapple, lettuce, and celery in a medium bowl. Just set it aside.

2. In a small bowl, make the dressing. Mix the mayonnaise, Tabasco sauce, pepper, and lemon juice.

3. Use the chicken mixture to add the dressing and stir until well-mixed.

Per serving: Calories: 310kcal; Fat: 23g; Carbs: 9g; Protein: 17g; Phosphorus: 134mg; Sodium: 200mg; Potassium: 260mg

42. Grapes Jicama Salad

Preparation time: 5 minutes
Cooking time: 0 minutes
Servings: 2
Ingredients:

• 1 jicama, peeled and sliced
• 1 carrot, sliced
• 1/2 medium red onion, sliced
• 1 ¼ cup seedless grapes
• 1/3 cup fresh basil leaves
• 1 tablespoon apple cider vinegar
• 1 ½ tablespoon lemon juice
• 1 ½ tablespoon lime juice

Directions:

1. Put all the salad ingredients into a suitable salad bowl.

2. Toss them well and refrigerate for 1 hour.

3. Serve.

Per serving: Calories: 203kcal; Fat: 1g; Carbs: 25g; Protein: 4g; Phosphorus: 141mg; Sodium: 44mg; Potassium: 429mg

43. Italian Cucumber Salad

Preparation time: 5 minutes
Cooking time: 0 minutes
Servings: 2
Ingredients:

• 1/4 cup rice vinegar
• 1/8 teaspoon stevia
• 1/2 teaspoon olive oil
• 1/8 teaspoon black pepper
• 1/2 cucumber, sliced
• 1 cup carrots, sliced
• 2 tablespoons green onion, sliced
• 2 tablespoons red bell pepper, sliced
• 1/2 teaspoon Italian seasoning blend

Directions:

1. Put all the salad ingredients into a suitable salad bowl.

2. Toss them well and refrigerate for 1 hour.

3. Serve.

Per serving: Calories: 112kcal; Fat: 2g; Carbs: 23g; Protein: 3g; Phosphorus: 198mg; Sodium: 43mg; Potassium: 529mg

44. Salmon & Pesto Salad

Preparation time: 5 minutes

Cooking time: 15 minutes

Servings: 2

Ingredients:

• For the pesto:
• 1 minced garlic clove
• ½ cup fresh arugula
• ¼ cup extra virgin olive oil
• ½ cup fresh basil
• 1 tsp black pepper
• For the salmon:
• 4 oz. skinless salmon fillet
• 1 tbsp. coconut oil
• For the salad:
• ½ juiced lemon
• 2 sliced radishes
• ½ cup iceberg lettuce
• 1 tsp black pepper

Directions:

1. Prepare the pesto by blending all the fixing for the pesto in a food processor or grinding with a pestle and mortar. Set aside.

2. Add a skillet to the stove on medium-high heat and melt the coconut oil. Add the salmon to the pan. Cook for 7-8 minutes and turn over.

3. Cook within 3-4 minutes or until cooked through. Remove fillets from the skillet and allow them to rest.

4. Mix the lettuce and the radishes and squeeze over the juice of ½ lemon. Shred the salmon using a fork and mixed through the salad. Toss to coat and sprinkle with a bit of black pepper to serve.

Per serving: Calories: 221kcal; Fat: 34g; Carbs: 1g; Protein: 13g; Phosphorus: 258mg; Sodium: 80mg; Potassium: 119mg

45. Butterscotch Apple Salad

Preparation time: 5 minutes

Cooking time: 0 minutes

Servings: 6

Ingredients:

• 3 cups jazz apples, chopped
• 8 oz. canned crushed pineapple
• 8 oz. whipped topping
• 1/2 cup butterscotch topping
• 1/3 cup almonds
• 1/4 cup butterscotch

Directions:

1. Put all the salad ingredients into a suitable salad bowl.

2. Toss them well and refrigerate for 1 hour.

3. Serve.

Per serving: Calories: 293kcal; Fat: 13g; Carbs: 18g; Protein: 4g; Phosphorus: 202mg; Sodium: 52mg; Potassium: 296mg

46. Carrot Jicama Salad

Preparation time: 5 minutes
Cooking time: 0 minutes
Servings: 2
Ingredients:

- 2 cup carrots, julienned
- 1 1/2 cups jicama, julienned
- 2 tablespoons lime juice
- 1 tablespoon olive oil
- ½ tablespoon apple cider
- ½ teaspoon brown Swerve

Directions:

1. Put all the salad ingredients into a suitable salad bowl.
2. Toss them well and refrigerate for 1 hour.
3. Serve.

Per serving: Calories: 173kcal; Fat: 7g; Carbs: 31g; Protein: 2g; Phosphorus: 96mg; Sodium: 80mg; Potassium: 501mg

47. Thai Cucumber Salad

Preparation time: 5 minutes
Cooking time: 5 minutes
Servings: 2
Ingredients:

- ¼ cup chopped peanuts
- ¼ cup white sugar
- ½ cup cilantro
- ¼ cup rice wine vinegar
- 3 cucumbers
- 2 jalapeno peppers

Directions:

1. Add all ingredients in a small basin and combine well
2. Serve with dressing

Per serving: Calories: 20kcal; Fat: 0g; Carbs: 5g; Protein: 1g; Phosphorus: 47mg; Sodium: 85mg; Potassium: 190mg

48. Korean Pear Salad

Preparation time: 5 minutes
Cooking time: 15 minutes
Servings: 2
Ingredients:

- 6 cups green lettuce
- 4 medium-sized pears (peeled, cored, and diced)
- ½ cup of sugar
- ½ cup of pecan nuts
- ½ cup of water
- 2 oz of blue cheese
- ½ cup of cranberries
- ½ cup of dressing

Directions:

1. Dissolve the water and sugar in a frying pan (non-stick).
2. Heat the mixture until it turns into syrup, and then add the nuts immediately.
3. Place the syrup on parchment paper and separate the nuts while the mixture is hot. Let it cool down.
4. Prepare lettuce in a salad bowl and add the pears, blue cheese, and cranberries to the salad.
5. Add the caramelized nuts to the salad and serve it with a dressing of choice on the side.

Per serving: Calories: 112kcal; Fat: 9g; Carbs: 6g; Protein: 2g; Phosphorus: 72mg; Sodium: 130mg; Potassium: 160mg

49. Panzanella Salad

Preparation time: 10 minutes

Cooking time: 5 minutes

Servings: 4

Ingredients:

• 2 cucumbers, chopped

• 1 red onion, sliced

• 2 red bell peppers, chopped

• ¼ cup fresh cilantro, chopped

• 1 tablespoon capers

• 1 oz whole-grain bread, chopped

• 1 tablespoon canola oil

• ½ teaspoon minced garlic

• 1 tablespoon Dijon mustard

• 1 teaspoon olive oil

• 1 teaspoon lime juice

Directions:

1. Pour canola oil into the skillet, then bring it to a boil.

2. Add chopped bread and roast it until crunchy (3-5 minutes).

3. Meanwhile, in the salad bowl, combine sliced red onion, cucumbers, bell peppers, cilantro, and capers, and mix up gently.

4. Make the dressing: Mix lime juice, olive oil, Dijon mustard, and minced garlic.

5. Put the dressing over the salad and stir it directly before serving.

Per serving: Calories: 224kcal; Fat: 10g; Carbs: 26g; Protein: 7g; Phosphorus: 84mg; Sodium: 401mg; Potassium: 325mg

50. Grated Carrot Salad with Lemon-Dijon Vinaigrette

Preparation time: 15 minutes

Cooking time: 10 minutes

Servings: 8 servings

Ingredients:

• 9 small carrots (14 cm), peeled

• 2 tbsp. 1/2 teaspoon Dijon mustard

• 1 C. lemon juice

• 2 tbsp. extra virgin olive oil

• 1-2 tsp. honey (to taste)

• ¼ tsp. salt

• ¼ tsp. freshly ground pepper (to taste)

• 2 tbsp. chopped parsley

• One green onion, thinly sliced

Directions:

1. Grate the carrots in a food processor.

2. Mix Dijon mustard, lemon juice, honey, olive oil, salt, and pepper in a salad bowl. Add the carrots, fresh parsley, and green onions. Stir to coat well. Cover and refrigerate until ready to be served.

Per serving: Calories: 61kcal; Fat: 4g; Carbs: 7g; Protein: 1g; Phosphorus: 22mg; Sodium: 88mg; Potassium: 197mg

51. Cucumber Couscous Salad

Preparation time: 5 minutes

Cooking time: 0 minutes

Servings: 4

Ingredients:

- 1 cucumber, sliced
- ½ cup red bell pepper, sliced
- ¼ cup sweet onion, sliced
- ¼ cup parsley, chopped
- ½ cup couscous, cooked
- 2 tablespoons olive oil
- 2 tablespoons rice vinegar
- 2 tablespoons feta cheese crumbled
- 1 ½ teaspoons dried basil
- 1/4 teaspoon black pepper

Directions:

1. Put all the salad ingredients into a suitable salad bowl.

2. Toss them well and refrigerate for 1 hour.

3. Serve.

Per serving: Calories: 202kcal; Fat: 10g; Carbs: 32g; Protein: 6g; Phosphorus: 192mg; Sodium: 258mg; Potassium: 209mg

52. Sesame Cucumber Salad

Preparation time: 5 minutes

Cooking time: 0 minute

Servings: 2

Ingredients:

- Cucumbers, thinly sliced – 1
- Sesame seeds - .5 teaspoon
- Rice wine vinegar – 1 tablespoon
- Sugar - .5 tablespoon
- Sesame seed oil – 1.5 tablespoons
- Red pepper flakes - .25 teaspoon

Directions:

1. You want the cucumbers sliced as thinly as you can get them. While you can certainly do this with a knife, it is quicker and easier if you use a mandolin.

2. Whisk together the sesame seeds, rice wine vinegar, sugar, sesame seed oil, and red pepper flakes in a medium to a small bowl. Once well combined, add in the cucumbers and toss the vegetables in the vinaigrette. Serve immediately.

Per serving: Calories: 92kcal; Fat: 5g; Carbs: 34g; Protein: 1g; Phosphorus: 46mg; Sodium: 117mg; Potassium: 250mg

53. Fruity Zucchini Salad

Preparation time: 5 minutes

Cooking time: 5 minutes

Servings: 4 servings

Ingredients:

- 400g zucchini
- 1 small onion
- 4 tbsp. olive oil
- 100g pineapple preserve, drained
- Salt, paprika
- thyme

Directions:

1. Dice the onions and sauté in the oil until translucent.

2. Cut the zucchini into slices and add—season with salt, paprika, and thyme.

3. Let cool and mix with the cut pineapple.

Per serving: Calories: 150kcal; Fat: 10g; Carbs: 10g; Protein: 2g; Phosphorus: 24mg; Sodium: 28mg; Potassium: 220mg

54. Tuna Macaroni Salad

Preparation time: 5 minutes

Cooking time: 25 minutes

Servings: 10 servings

Ingredients:

- 1 1/2 cups Uncooked Macaroni
- 1 170g Can of tuna in water
- 1/4 cup Mayonnaise
- Two medium celery stalks, diced
- 1 Tbsp. Lemon Pepper Seasoning

Directions:

1. Cook the pasta and let it cool in the refrigerator.

2. Drain the tuna in a colander and rinse it with cold water.

3. Add the tuna and celery once the macaroni has cooled.

4. Stir in mayonnaise and sprinkle with lemon seasoning. Mix well. Serve cold.

Per serving: Calories: 136kcal; Fat: 4g; Carbs: 18g; Protein: 8g; Phosphorus: 90mg; Sodium: 75mg; Potassium: 124mg

55. Couscous Salad

Preparation time: 5 minutes

Cooking time: 5 minutes

Servings: 5 servings

Ingredients:

- 3 cups of water
- 1/2 tsp. cinnamon tea
- 1/2 tsp. cumin tea
- 1 tsp. honey soup
- 2 tbsp. lemon juice
- 3 cups quick-cooking couscous
- 2 tbsp. tea of olive oil
- 1 green onion,
- Finely chopped 1 small carrot, finely diced
- 1/2 red pepper,
- Finely diced fresh coriander

Directions:

1. Stir in the water with the cinnamon, cumin, honey, and lemon juice and bring to a boil. Put the couscous in it, cover it, and remove it from the heat. To swell the couscous, stir with a fork. Add the vegetables, fresh herbs, and olive oil. It is possible to serve the salad warm or cold.

Per serving: Calories: 190kcal; Fat: 1g; Carbs: 38g; Protein: 6g; Phosphorus: 82mg; Sodium: 4mg; Potassium: 116mg

56. Green Tuna Salad

Preparation time: 10 minutes

Cooking time: 15 -20 minutes

Servings: 2

Ingredients:

- 5 ounces of tuna (in freshwater only)
- 2-3 cups of lettuce
- 1 cup of baby marrow
- 1/2 cup of red bell pepper
- 1/4 cup of red onion
- 1/4 cup of fresh thyme
- 2 tbsp olive oil
- 1/8 tsp of black pepper
- 2 tbsp of red wine vinegar

Directions:

1. Chop the bell pepper, onion, baby marrow, and thyme into small pieces.

2. Add a 3/4 cup of water to a saucepan and add the bell pepper, onion, baby marrow, and thyme to the pan. Let it boil, and steam the vegetables by adding a lid on top of the saucepan—steam for 10 minutes.

3. Remove the vegetables and drain them.

4. Combine the vegetables (once cooled down) with the chopped tomatoes and tuna.

5. Mix olive oil, red wine vinegar, and black pepper to create a salad dressing.

6. Add the mixture to a bed of lettuce and drizzle the dressing on top.

Per serving: Calories: 210kcal; Fat: 2g; Carbs: 4g; Protein: 43g; Phosphorus: 296mg; Sodium: 726mg; Potassium: 582mg

57. Chestnut Noodle Salad

Preparation time: 5 minutes
Cooking time: 0 minutes
Servings: 6
Ingredients:

- 8 cups cabbage, shredded
- 1/2 cup canned chestnuts, sliced
- 6 green onions, chopped
- 1/4 cup olive oil
- 1/4 cup apple cider vinegar
- 3/4 teaspoon stevia
- 1/8 teaspoon black pepper
- 1 cup chow Mein noodles, cooked

Directions:

1. Take a suitable salad bowl.

2. Start tossing in all the ingredients.

3. Mix well and serve.

Per serving: Calories: 191kcal; Fat: 13g; Carbs: 34g; Protein: 4g; Phosphorus: 188mg; Sodium: 78mg; Potassium: 302mg

58. Chicken Salad Balsamic

Preparation time: 15 minutes
Cooking time: 15 minutes
Servings: 6
Ingredients:

- 3 cups diced cold, cooked chicken
- 1 cup diced apple
- 1/2 cup diced celery
- 2 green onions, chopped
- 1/2 cup chopped walnuts
- 3 tablespoons. Balsamic vinegar
- 5 tablespoons. Olive oil
- Salt and pepper to taste

Directions:

1. Toss the celery, chicken, onion, walnuts, and apple in a big bowl.

2. Whisk the oil together with the vinegar in a small bowl. Pour the dressing over the salad. Then add pepper and salt to taste. Combine the ingredients thoroughly. Leave the mixture for 10-15 minutes. Toss once more and chill.

Per serving: Calories: 336kcal; Fat: 27g; Carbs: 6g; Protein: 19g; Phosphorus: 176mg; Sodium: 58mg; Potassium: 214mg

59. Farmer's Salad

Preparation time: 5 minutes
Cooking time: 5 minutes
Servings: 2 servings

Ingredients:

- 60g mixed-leaf salads
- 100g red pepper, diced
- 200g green beans
- 60g feta cheese
- 1 tbsp. wine vinegar
- 1 tbsp. diced onions
- Salt, pepper, sugar
- 2 tbsp. olive oil

Directions:

1. Mix vinegar with onions, oil, and spices with the salad.

2. Cut the sheep's cheese into cubes and serve with the salad. It goes well with baguette or flatbread with herb butter.

Per serving: Calories: 187kcal; Fat: 16g; Carbs: 4g; Protein: 8g; Phosphorus: 170mg; Sodium: 188mg; Potassium: 396mg

60. Cucumber Salad

Preparation time: 5 minutes

Cooking time: 5 minutes

Servings: 4

Ingredients:

- 1 tbsp. dried dill
- 1 onion
- ¼ cup water
- 1 cup vinegar
- 3 cucumbers
- ¾ cup white sugar

Directions:

1. In a bowl, add all ingredients, then mix well.

2. Serve with dressing.

Per serving: Calories: 49kcal; Fat: 0g; Carbs: 11g; Protein: 1g; Phosphorus: 24mg; Sodium: 341mg; Potassium: 171mg

Meat

61. Grilled Chicken Pizza

Preparation time: 20 minutes

Cooking time: 15 minutes

Servings: 2

Ingredients:

- 2 pita bread
- 3 tbsp. low sodium BBQ sauce
- 1/4 bowl red onion
- 4 oz. cooked chicken
- 2 tbsp. crumbled feta cheese
- 1/8 tsp. garlic powder

Directions:

1. Preheat oven to 350°F (that is 175°C).

2. Place two pitas on the pan after you have put non-stick cooking spray on it.

3. Spread BBQ sauce (2 tablespoons) on the pita.

4. Cut the onion and put it on the pita. Cube chicken and put it on the pitas.

5. Put both feta and garlic powder over the pita.

6. Bake for 12 minutes. Serve and enjoy!

Per serving: Calories: 320kcal; Fat: 6g; Carbs: 26g; Protein: 22g; Phosphorus: 220mg; Sodium: 520mg; Potassium: 250mg

62. Grilled Chicken

Preparation time: 15 minutes

Cooking time: 41 minutes

Servings: 8

Ingredients:

- 1 (3-inch) piece fresh ginger, minced
- 6 small garlic cloves, minced
- 1½ tablespoons tamarind paste
- 1 tablespoon organic honey
- ¼ cup coconut aminos
- 2½ tablespoons extra virgin olive oil
- 1½ tablespoons sesame oil, toasted
- ½ teaspoon ground cardamom
- Salt
- ground white pepper
- 1 (4-5-pound) whole chicken, cut into 8 pieces

Directions:

1. Mix all ingredients except chicken pieces in a large glass bowl. With a fork, pierce the chicken pieces thoroughly.

2. Add chicken pieces to bowl and coat with marinade generously. Cover and refrigerate to marinate for approximately a couple of hours overnight.

3. Preheat the grill to medium heat. Grease the grill grate. Place the chicken pieces on the grill, bone-side down. Grill, covered for approximately 20-25 minutes.

4. Change the side, grill, and cover for approximately 6-8 minutes. Change alongside it and grill, covered for about 5-8 minutes. Serve.

Per serving: Calories: 423kcal; Fat: 12g; Carbs: 20g; Protein: 42g; Phosphorus: 0mg; Sodium: 282mg; Potassium: 0mg

63. Beer Pork Ribs

Preparation time: 10 minutes

Cooking time: 8 hours

Servings: 1

Ingredients:

• 2 pounds of pork ribs, cut into two units/racks

• 18 oz. of root beer

• 2 cloves of garlic, minced

• 2 tbsp. of onion powder

• 2 tbsp. of vegetable oil (optional)

Directions:

1. Wrap the pork ribs with vegetable oil and place one unit on the bottom of your slow cooker with half of the minced garlic and the onion powder.

2. Place the other rack on top of the garlic and onion powder.

3. Pour over the root beer and cover the lid.

4. Let simmer for 8 hours on low heat.

5. Take off and finish optionally in a grilling pan for a nice sear.

Per serving: Calories: 301kcal; Fat: 18g; Carbs: 36g; Protein: 21g; Phosphorus: 209mg; Sodium: 729mg; Potassium: 200mg

64. Ground Turkey With Veggies

Preparation time: 15 minutes

Cooking time: 12 minutes

Servings: 4

Ingredients:

• 1 tablespoon sesame oil

• 1 tablespoon coconut oil

• 1-pound lean ground turkey

• 2 tablespoons fresh ginger, minced

• 2 minced garlic cloves

• 1 (16-ounce) bag of the vegetable mix (broccoli, carrot, cabbage, kale, and Brussels sprouts)

• ¼ cup coconut aminos

• 2 tablespoons balsamic vinegar

Directions:

1. In a big skillet, heat both oils on medium-high heat. Add turkey, ginger, and garlic and cook for approximately 5-6 minutes. Add vegetable mix and cook for about 4-5 minutes. Stir in coconut aminos and vinegar and cook for about 1 minute. Serve hot.

Per serving: Calories: 234kcal; Fat: 9g; Carbs: 9g; Protein: 29g; Phosphorus: 14mg; Sodium: 115mg; Potassium: 92mg

65. Creamy Chicken

Preparation time: 10 minutes

Cooking time: 15 minutes

Servings: 2

Ingredients:

• 3 tbsp. oil

• 2 pounds cut into 1-inch thick strips of skinless, boneless chicken breasts

• 4 minced garlic cloves

• ½ tsp. ground ginger

• ½ tsp. ground coriander

• ½ tsp. ground cumin

• ¼ tsp. crushed red pepper flakes

• ½ cup chicken broth

- 1/3 cup low-fat sour cream
- 1 tbsp. chopped fresh parsley

Directions:

1. In a large skillet, melt oil on medium-high heat.

2. Add chicken, then cook for about 5–6 minutes.

3. Add garlic and spices, then cook for 1 minute.

4. Add broth and bring to a boil. Reduce the heat to medium-low.

5. Simmer for about 5 minutes, stirring occasionally.

6. Stir in cream and simmer, occasionally stirring for about 3 minutes.

7. Serve hot with the garnishing of parsley.

Per serving: Calories: 206kcal; Fat: 11g; Carbs: 2g; Protein: 26g; Phosphorus: 58mg; Sodium: 144mg; Potassium: 43mg

66. Roasted Spatchcock Chicken

Preparation time: 20 minutes
Cooking time: 50 minutes
Servings: 4-6
Ingredients:

- 1 (4-pound) whole chicken
- 1 (1-inch) piece of fresh ginger, sliced
- 4 garlic cloves, chopped
- 1 small bunch of fresh thyme
- Pinch of cayenne
- Salt
- ground black pepper
- ¼ cup fresh lemon juice
- 3 tablespoons extra virgin olive oil

Directions:

1. Arrange chicken breast side down onto a large cutting board. With a kitchen shear, begin with the thigh, cut along one side of the backbone, and turn the chicken around.

2. Now, cut along sleep issues and discard the backbone. Change the inside and open it like a book. Flatten the backbone firmly to flatten.

3. Add all ingredients except chicken and pulse till smooth in a food processor. In a big baking dish, add the marinade mixture.

4. Add chicken and coat with marinade generously. With plastic wrap, cover the baking dish and refrigerate to marinate overnight.

5. Preheat the oven to 450 degrees F. Arrange a rack in a very roasting pan. Remove the chicken from the refrigerator onto a rack over the roasting pan, skin side down. Roast for about 50 minutes, turning once in the middle way.

Per serving: Calories: 419kcal; Fat: 14g; Carbs: 28g; Protein: 40g; Phosphorus: 166mg; Sodium: 68mg; Potassium: 196mg

67. Red And Green Grapes Chicken Salad with Curry

Preparation time: 5 minutes
Cooking time: 0 minute
Servings: 2
Ingredients:

- 1 apple
- 1/4 bowl of seedless red grapes
- 1/4 bowl of seedless green grapes
- 4 cooked skinless and boneless chicken breasts

- 1 piece celery
- 1/2 bowl onion
- 1/2 bowl canned water chestnuts
- 1/2 tsp. curry powder
- 3/4 cup mayonnaise
- 1/8 tsp. black pepper

Directions:

1. Cut the chicken into small dices and chop celery, onion, and apple. Drain and cut chestnuts.

2. Put together the chicken pieces, celery, onion, apple, grapes, water chestnuts, pepper, curry powder, and mayonnaise.

3. Serve it in a big salad bowl. Enjoy!

Per serving: Calories: 235kcal; Fat: 4g; Carbs: 23g; Protein: 13g; Phosphorus: 114mg; Sodium: 160mg; Potassium: 200mg

68. Chicken Breast And Bok Choy

Preparation time: 10 minutes

Cooking time: 30 minutes

Servings: 4

Ingredients:

- 4 slices lemon
- Pepper, to taste
- 4 chicken breasts, boneless and skinless
- 1 tbsp. Dijon mustard
- 1 small leek, thinly sliced
- 2 julienned carrots
- 2 cups thinly sliced book Choy
- 1 tbsp. chopped thyme
- 1 tbsp. EVOO

Directions:

1. Start by setting your oven to 425°F.

2. Mix the thyme, olive oil, and mustard in a small bowl.

3. Take four 18-inch-long pieces of parchment paper and fold them in half. Cut them like you would make a heart. Open each of the pieces and lay them flat.

4. In each parchment piece, place .5 cup of book Choy, a few slices of leek, and a small handful of carrots.

5. Lay the chicken breast on top and season with some pepper.

6. Brush the chicken breasts with the marinade and top each one with a slice of lemon.

7. Fold the packets and roll down the edges to seal the packages.

8. Allow them to cook for 20 minutes. Let them rest for 5 minutes, and make sure you open them carefully when serving. Enjoy!

Per serving: Calories: 164kcal; Fat: 3g; Carbs: 21g; Protein: 24g; Phosphorus: 26mg; Sodium: 256mg; Potassium: 189mg

69. Ground Turkey With Asparagus

Preparation time: 15 minutes

Cooking time: 15 minutes

Servings: 8

Ingredients:

- 1¾ pound lean ground turkey
- 2 tablespoons sesame oil
- 1 medium onion, chopped
- 1 cup celery, chopped
- 6 garlic cloves, minced
- 2 cups asparagus, cut into 1-inch pieces

- 1/3 cup coconut aminos
- 2½ teaspoons ginger powder
- 2 tablespoons organic coconut crystals
- 1 tablespoon arrowroot starch
- 1 tablespoon cold water
- ¼ teaspoon red pepper flakes, crushed

Directions:

1. Heat a substantial nonstick skillet on medium-high heat. Add turkey and cook for approximately 5-7 minutes or till browned. Transfer the turkey inside a bowl with a slotted spoon and discard the grease from the skillet.

2. Heat-up oil on medium heat in the same skillet. Add onion, celery, and garlic and sauté for about 5 minutes. Add asparagus and cooked turkey, minimizing the temperature to medium-low.

3. Meanwhile, mix coconut aminos, ginger powder, and coconut crystals n medium heat and convey some boil inside a pan.

4. Mix arrowroot starch and water in a smaller bowl. Slowly add arrowroot mixture, stirring continuously. Cook for approximately 2-3 minutes.

5. Add the sauce to the skillet with the turkey mixture and stir to blend. Stir in red pepper flakes and cook for approximately 2-3 minutes. Serve hot.

Per serving: Calories: 309kcal; Fat: 20g; Carbs: 19g; Protein: 28g; Phosphorus: 0mg; Sodium: 78mg; Potassium: 196mg

70. Curried Chicken With Cauliflower

Preparation time: 20 minutes
Cooking time: 2 hours and 30 minutes
Servings: 6
Ingredients:

- Lime juice 2 limes
- 1/2 tsp. dried oregano
- Cauliflower head, cut into florets
- 4 tsp. EVOO, divided
- 6 chicken thighs, bone-in
- 1/2 tsp. pepper, divided
- 1/4 tsp. paprika
- 1/2 tsp. ground cumin
- 3 tbsp. curry powder

Directions:

1. Mix a quarter of a tsp. of pepper, paprika, cumin, and curry in a small bowl.

2. Add the chicken thighs to a medium bowl, drizzle with 2 tsp. of olive oil, and sprinkle in the curry mixture.

3. Toss them together so that the chicken is well coated.

4. Cover this up and refrigerate it for at least 2 hours.

5. Now set your oven to 400°F.

6. Toss the cauliflower, remaining oil, and oregano in a medium bowl. Arrange the cauliflower and chicken across a baking sheet in one layer.

7. Allow this to bake for 40 minutes. Stir the cauliflower and flip the chicken once during the cooking time. The chicken should be browned,

and the juices should run clear. The temperature of the chicken should reach 165°F.

8. Serve with some lime juice. Enjoy!

Per serving: Calories: 175kcal; Fat: 6g; Carbs: 23g; Protein: 16g; Phosphorus: 152mg; Sodium: 77mg; Potassium: 486mg

71. Ground Chicken With Basil

Preparation time: 15 minutes

Cooking time: 16 minutes

Servings: 8

Ingredients:

• 2 pounds lean ground chicken

• 3 tablespoons coconut oil, divided

• 1 zucchini, chopped

• 1 red bell pepper, seeded and chopped

• ½ of green bell pepper, seeded and chopped

• 4 garlic cloves, minced

• 1 (1-inch) piece fresh ginger, minced

• 1 (1-inch) piece of fresh turmeric, minced

• 1 fresh red chili, sliced thinly

• 1 tablespoon organic honey

• 1 tablespoon coconut aminos

• 1½ tablespoons fish sauce

• ½ cup fresh basil, chopped

• Salt

• ground black pepper

• 1 tablespoon fresh lime juice

Directions:

1. Heat a large skillet on medium-high heat. Add ground beef and cook for approximately 5 minutes or till browned completely.

2. Transfer the beef to a bowl. In a similar pan, melt 1 tablespoon coconut oil on medium-high heat. Add zucchini and bell peppers and stir fry for around 3-4 minutes.

3. Transfer the vegetables inside the bowl with the chicken. In the same pan, melt the remaining coconut oil on medium heat. Add garlic, ginger, turmeric, red chili and sauté for approximately 1-2 minutes.

4. Add chicken mixture, honey, and coconut aminos and increase the heat to high. Cook within 4-5 minutes or till sauce is nearly reduced. Stir in the remaining ingredients and take off the heat.

Per serving: Calories: 407kcal; Fat: 7g; Carbs: 20g; Protein: 36g; Phosphorus: 149mg; Sodium: 21mg; Potassium: 706mg

72. Roasted Chicken Breast

Preparation time: 15 minutes

Cooking time: 40 minutes

Servings: 4-6

Ingredients:

• ½ of a small apple, peeled, cored, and chopped

• 1 bunch of scallions, trimmed and chopped roughly

• 8 fresh ginger slices, chopped

• 2 garlic cloves, chopped

• 3 tablespoons essential olive oil

• 12 teaspoon sesame oil, toasted

• 3 tablespoons using apple cider vinegar

• 1 tablespoon fish sauce

• 1 tablespoon coconut aminos

- Salt
- ground black pepper
- 4-pounds chicken thighs

Directions:

1. Pulse all the fixing except chicken thighs in a blender. Transfer a combination and chicken into a large Ziploc bag and seal it.

2. Shake the bag to marinade well. Refrigerate to marinate for about 12 hours—warm oven to 400 degrees F. Arrange a rack on a foil paper-lined baking sheet.

3. Place the chicken thighs on the rack, skin-side down. Roast for about 40 minutes, flipping once within the middle way.

Per serving: Calories: 451kcal; Fat: 17g; Carbs: 277g; Protein: 42g; Phosphorus: 121mg; Sodium: 483mg; Potassium: 324mg

73. Grilled Chicken With Pineapple & Veggies

Preparation time: 20 or so minutes
Cooking time: 22 minutes
Servings: 4
Ingredients:

For Sauce:
- 1 garlic oil, minced
- ¾ teaspoon fresh ginger, minced
- ½ cup coconut aminos
- ¼ cup fresh pineapple juice
- 2 tablespoons freshly squeezed lemon juice
- 2 tablespoons balsamic vinegar
- ¼ teaspoon red pepper flakes, crushed
- Salt
- ground black pepper

For Grilling:
- 4 skinless, boneless chicken breasts
- 1 pineapple, peeled and sliced
- 1 bell pepper, seeded and cubed
- 1 zucchini, sliced
- 1red onion, sliced

Directions:

1. For sauce in a pan, mix all ingredients on medium-high heat. Bring to a boil reducing the heat to medium-low. Cook for approximately 5-6 minutes.

2. Remove, then keep aside to cool down slightly. Coat the chicken breasts about ¼ from the sauce. Keep aside for approximately half an hour.

3. Preheat the grill to medium-high heat. Grease the grill grate. Grill the chicken pieces for around 5-8 minutes per side.

4. Now, squeeze pineapple and vegetables on the grill grate. Grill the pineapple within 3 minutes per side. Grill the vegetables for approximately 4-5 minutes, stirring once inside the middle way.

5. Cut the chicken breasts into desired-size slices, and divide the chicken, pineapple, and vegetables into serving plates. Serve alongside the remaining sauce.

Per serving: Calories: 435kcal; Fat: 12g; Carbs: 25g; Protein: 38g; Phosphorus: 184mg; Sodium: 755mg; Potassium: 334mg

74. Chicken &Veggie Casserole

Preparation time: 15 minutes

Cooking time: 30 minutes

Servings: 4

Ingredients:

- 1/3 cup Dijon mustard
- 1/3 cup organic honey
- 1 teaspoon dried basil
- ¼ teaspoon ground turmeric
- 1 teaspoon dried basil, crushed
- Salt
- ground black pepper
- 1¾ pound chicken breasts
- 1 cup fresh white mushrooms, sliced
- ½ head broccoli, cut into small florets

Directions:

1. Warm oven to 350 degrees F. Lightly greases a baking dish. Mix all ingredients except chicken, mushrooms, and broccoli in a bowl.

2. Put the chicken in your prepared baking dish, then top with mushroom slices. Place broccoli florets around the chicken evenly.

3. Pour 1 / 2 of the honey mixture over the chicken and broccoli. Bake for approximately 20 minutes. Now, coat the chicken with the remaining sauce and bake for about 10 minutes.

Per serving: Calories: 427kcal; Fat: 9g; Carbs: 16g; Protein: 35g; Phosphorus: 353mg; Sodium: 1mg; Potassium: 529mg

75. Chicken Meatloaf With Veggies

Preparation time: 20 minutes

Cooking time: 1-1¼ hours

Servings: 4

Ingredients:

- For Meatloaf:
- ½ cup cooked chickpeas
- 2 egg whites
- 2½ teaspoons poultry seasoning
- Salt
- ground black pepper
- 10-ounce lean ground chicken
- 1 cup red bell pepper, seeded and minced
- 1 cup celery stalk, minced
- 1/3 cup steel-cut oats
- 1 cup tomato puree, divided
- 2 tablespoons dried onion flakes, crushed
- 1 tablespoon prepared mustard
- For Veggies:
- 2-pounds summer squash, sliced
- 16-ounce frozen Brussels sprouts
- 2 tablespoons extra-virgin extra virgin olive oil
- Salt
- ground black pepper

Directions:

1. Warm oven to 350 degrees F. Grease a 9x5-inch loaf pan. Add chickpeas, egg whites, poultry seasoning, salt, and black pepper in a mixer and pulse till smooth.

2. Transfer a combination to a large bowl. Add chicken, veggies, oats, ½ cup of tomato puree, and onion flakes and mix till well combined.

3. Transfer the amalgamation into the prepared loaf pan evenly. With both hands, press down the amalgamation slightly.

4. In another bowl, mix mustard and remaining tomato puree. Place the mustard mixture over the loaf pan evenly.

5. Bake for approximately 1-1¼ hours or till the desired doneness. Meanwhile, in a big pan of water, arrange a steamer basket. Cover and steam for about 10-12 minutes. Drain well and aside.

6. Now, prepare the Brussels sprouts according to the package's directions. Add veggies, oil, salt, and black pepper in a big bowl and toss to coat well. Serve the meatloaf with veggies.

Per serving: Calories: 420kcal; Fat: 9g; Carbs: 21g; Protein: 36g; Phosphorus: 237mg; Sodium: 136mg; Potassium: 583mg

Fish and Seafood

76. Haddock &Oiled Leeks

Preparation time: 5 minutes

Cooking time: 15 minutes

Servings: 2

Ingredients:

• 1 tbsp. oil

• 1 sliced leek

• ¼ tsp. black pepper

• 2 tsp. Chopped parsley

• 6 oz. haddock fillets

• ½ juiced lemon.

Directions:

1. Preheat the oven to 375 deg. F/Gas Mark 5.

2. Add the haddock fillets to baking or parchment paper and sprinkle with black pepper.

3. Squeeze over the lemon juice and wrap it into a parcel.

4. Bake the parcel on a baking tray for 10-15 minutes or until the fish is thoroughly cooked.

5. Meanwhile, heat the oil over medium-low heat in a small pan.

6. Add the leeks and parsley, and sauté for 5-7 minutes until soft.

7. Serve the haddock fillets on a bed of oiled leeks, and enjoy!

Per serving: Calories: 124kcal; Fat: 7g; Carbs: 0g; Protein: 15g; Phosphorus: 220mg; Sodium: 161mg; Potassium: 251mg

77. Four-Ingredients Salmon Fillet

Preparation time: 5 minutes

Cooking time: 25 minutes

Servings: 1

Ingredients:

• 4 oz. salmon fillet

• ½ teaspoon salt

• 1 teaspoon sesame oil

• ½ teaspoon sage

Directions:

1. Rub the fillet with salt and sage. Put the fish in the tray, then sprinkle it with sesame oil. Cook the fish for 25 minutes at 365F. Flip the fish carefully onto another side after 12 minutes of cooking. Serve.

Per serving: Calories: 191kcal; Fat: 12g; Carbs: 0g; Protein: 22g; Phosphorus: 472mg; Sodium: 70mg; Potassium: 636mg

78. Saucy Fish Dill

Preparation time: 5 minutes

Cooking time: 15 minutes

Servings: 4

Ingredients:

• 4 (4 oz.) salmon fillets

Dill Sauce:

• 1 cup whipped cream

• 4 minced garlic cloves

• ½ small onion, diced

• 3 tablespoons fresh or dried dill (as desired)

• ½ teaspoon ground pepper

- 1 teaspoon Mrs. Dash (optional)
- 2 drops of hot sauce (optional)

Directions:

1. Place the salmon fillets in a moderately shallow baking tray.

2. Whisk the cream and all the dill-sauce ingredients in a bowl.

3. Spread the dill sauce over the fillets liberally.

4. Cover the fillet pan with a foil sheet and bake for 15 minutes at 350 degrees F.

5. Serve warm.

Per serving: Calories: 432kcal; Fat: 27g; Carbs: 5g; Protein: 36g; Phosphorus: 265mg; Sodium: 280mg; Potassium: 590mg

79. Spanish Cod In Sauce

Preparation time: 10 minutes

Cooking time: 5 1/2 hours

Servings: 2

Ingredients:

- 1 teaspoon tomato paste
- 1 teaspoon garlic, diced
- 1 white onion, sliced
- 1 jalapeno pepper, chopped
- 1/3 cup chicken stock
- 7 oz. Spanish cod fillet
- 1 teaspoon paprika
- 1 teaspoon salt

Directions:

1. Pour chicken stock into the saucepan. Add tomato paste and mix up the liquid until homogenous. Add garlic, onion, jalapeno pepper, paprika, and salt.

2. Bring the liquid to a boil, then simmer it. Chop the cod fillet and add it to the tomato liquid. Simmer the fish for 10 minutes over low heat. Serve the fish in bowls with tomato sauce.

Per serving: Calories: 113kcal; Fat: 2g; Carbs: 7g; Protein: 29g; Phosphorus: 18mg; Sodium: 597mg; Potassium: 659mg

80. Salmon Baked In Foil With Fresh Thyme

Preparation time: 10 minutes

Cooking time: 30 minutes

Servings: 4

Ingredients:

- 4 fresh thyme sprigs
- 4 garlic cloves, peeled, roughly chopped
- 16 oz. salmon fillets (4 oz. each fillet)
- ½ teaspoon salt
- ½ teaspoon ground black pepper
- 4 tablespoons cream
- 4 teaspoons oil
- ¼ teaspoon cumin seeds

Directions:

1. Line the baking tray with foil. Sprinkle the fish fillets with salt, ground black pepper, and cumin seeds, and arrange them in the tray with oil.

2. Add thyme sprig on the top of every fillet. Then add cream, oil, and garlic. Bake the fish for 30 minutes at 345F. Serve.

Per serving: Calories: 198kcal; Fat: 11g; Carbs: 2g; Protein: 23g; Phosphorus: 425mg; Sodium: 366mg; Potassium: 661mg

81. Oregon Tuna Patties

Preparation time: 10 minutes

Cooking time: 15 minutes

Servings: 4

Ingredients:

- 1 (14.75 ounces) can of tuna
- 2 tablespoons oil
- 1 medium onion, chopped
- 2/3 cup graham cracker crumbs
- 2 egg whites, beaten
- 1/4 cup chopped fresh parsley
- 1 teaspoon dry mustard
- 3 tablespoons olive oil.

Directions:

1. Drain the tuna, reserving 3/4 cup of the liquid. Flake the meat. Melt oil in a large skillet over medium-high heat. Add onion, and cook until tender. In a medium bowl, combine the onions with the reserved tuna liquid, 1/3 of the graham cracker crumbs, egg whites, parsley, mustard, and tuna.

Per serving: Calories: 204kcal; Fat: 6g; Carbs: 34g; Protein: 11g; Phosphorus: 106mg; Sodium: 111mg; Potassium: 164mg

82. Poached Halibut In Mango Sauce

Preparation time: 10 minutes

Cooking time: 10 minutes

Servings: 4

Ingredients:

- 1-pound halibut
- 1/3 cup oil
- 1 rosemary sprig
- ½ teaspoon ground black pepper
- 1 teaspoon salt
- 1 teaspoon honey
- ¼ cup of mango juice
- 1 teaspoon cornstarch

Directions:

1. Put oil in the saucepan and melt it. Add rosemary sprig. Sprinkle the halibut with salt and ground black pepper. Put the fish in the boiling oil and poach it for 4 minutes.

2. Meanwhile, pour mango juice into the skillet. Add honey and bring the liquid to a boil. Add cornstarch and whisk until the liquid starts to be thick. Then remove it from the heat.

3. Transfer the poached halibut to the plate and cut it on 4. Place every fish serving on the serving plate and top with mango sauce.

Per serving: Calories: 349kcal; Fat: 29g; Carbs: 3g; Protein: 18g; Phosphorus: 154mg; Sodium: 29mg; Potassium: 388mg

83. Chili Mussels

Preparation time: 7 minutes

Cooking time: 10 minutes

Servings: 4

Ingredients:

- 1-pound mussels
- 1 chili pepper, chopped
- 1 cup chicken stock
- ½ cup almond milk
- 1 teaspoon olive oil
- 1 teaspoon minced garlic
- 1 teaspoon ground coriander

- ½ teaspoon salt
- 1 cup fresh parsley, chopped
- 4 tablespoons lemon juice

Directions:

1. Pour almond milk into the saucepan. Add chili pepper, chicken stock, olive oil, minced garlic, ground coriander, salt, and lemon juice.

2. Bring the liquid to a boil and add mussels. Boil the mussel for 4 minutes or until they will open shells. Then add chopped parsley and mix up the meal well. Remove it from the heat.

Per serving: Calories: 136kcal; Fat: 5g; Carbs: 8g; Protein: 15g; Phosphorus: 181mg; Sodium: 320mg; Potassium: 312mg

84. Oven-Fried Southern-Style Catfish

Preparation time: 10 minutes
Cooking time: 35 minutes
Servings: 4
Ingredients:

- 1 egg white
- ½ cup of all-purpose flour
- ¼ cup of cornmeal
- ¼ cup of panko bread crumbs
- 1 teaspoon of salt-free Cajun seasoning
- 1 pound of catfish fillets

Directions:

1. Heat oven to 450° F

2. Use cooking spray to spray a non-stick baking sheet

3. Using a bowl, beat the egg white until very soft peaks are formed. Don't over-beat

4. Use a sheet of wax paper and place the flour over it

5. Using a different sheet of wax paper to combine and mix the cornmeal, panko and the Cajun seasoning

6. Cut the catfish fillet into four pieces, then dip the fish in the flour, shaking off the excess

7. Dip coated fish in the egg white, rolling into the cornmeal mixture

8. Place the fish on the baking pan. Repeat with the remaining fish fillets

9. Use cooking spray to spray over the fish fillets. Bake for about 10 to 12 minutes or until the sides of the fillets become browned and crisp

Per serving: Calories: 250kcal; Fat: 10g; Carbs: 19g; Protein: 22g; Phosphorus: 262mg; Sodium: 124mg; Potassium: 401mg

85. Broiled Salmon Fillets

Preparation time: 5 minutes
Cooking time: 10 minutes
Servings: 4
Ingredients:

- 1 tablespoon ginger root, grated
- 1 clove garlic, minced
- ¼ cup maple syrup
- 1 tablespoon hot pepper sauce
- 4 salmon fillets, skinless

Directions:

1. Grease a pan with cooking spray and place it over moderate heat.

2. Add the ginger and garlic, and sauté for 3 minutes, then transfer to a bowl.

3. Add the hot pepper sauce and maple syrup to the ginger-garlic.

4. Mix well and keep this mixture aside.

5. Place the salmon fillet in a suitable baking tray, greased with cooking oil.

6. Brush the maple sauce over the fillets liberally

7. Broil them for 10 minutes in the oven at broiler settings.

8. Serve warm.

Per serving: Calories: 289kcal; Fat: 11g; Carbs: 13g; Protein: 34g; Phosphorus: 230mg; Sodium: 80mg; Potassium: 331mg

86. Fish Chili With Lentils

Preparation time: 10 minutes
Cooking time: 30 minutes
Servings: 4
Ingredients:

- 1 red pepper, chopped
- 1 yellow onion, diced
- 1 teaspoon ground black pepper
- 1 teaspoon butter
- 1 jalapeno pepper, chopped
- ½ cup lentils
- 3 cups chicken stock
- 1 teaspoon salt
- 1 tablespoon tomato paste
- 1 teaspoon chili pepper
- 3 tablespoons fresh cilantro, chopped
- 8 oz. cod, chopped

Directions:

1. Place butter, red pepper, onion, and ground black pepper in the saucepan. Roast the vegetables for 5 minutes over medium heat.

2. Then add chopped jalapeno pepper, lentils, and chili pepper. Mix up the mixture well and add chicken stock and tomato paste. Stir until homogenous. Add cod. Close the lid and cook chili for 20 minutes over medium heat.

Per serving: Calories: 187kcal; Fat: 2g; Carbs: 21g; Protein: 21g; Phosphorus: 50mg; Sodium: 44mg; Potassium: 281mg

87. Herbed Vegetable Trout

Preparation time: 3 minutes
Cooking time: 12 minutes
Servings: 4
Ingredients:

- 14 oz. trout fillets
- 1/2 teaspoon herb seasoning blend
- 1 lemon, sliced
- 2 green onions, sliced
- 1 stalk celery, chopped
- 1 medium carrot, julienne

Directions:

1. Prepare and preheat a charcoal grill over moderate heat.

2. Place the trout fillets over a large piece of foil and drizzle herb seasoning on top.

3. Spread the lemon slices, carrots, celery, and green onions over the fish.

4. Cover the fish with foil and pack it.

5. Place the packed fish on the grill and cook for 15 minutes.

6. Once done, remove the foil from the fish.

7. Serve.

Per serving: Calories: 202kcal; Fat: 9g; Carbs: 4g; Protein: 18g; Phosphorus: 287mg; Sodium: 82mg; Potassium: 560mg

88. Grilled Lemony Cod

Preparation time: 3 minutes

Cooking time: 10 minutes

Servings: 4

Ingredients:

- 1 lb. cod fillets
- 1 teaspoon salt-free lemon pepper seasoning
- 1/4 cup lemon juice

Directions:

1. Rub the cod fillets with lemon pepper seasoning and lemon juice.

2. Grease a baking tray with cooking spray and place the salmon in the baking tray.

3. Bake the fish for 10 minutes at 350 degrees F in a preheated oven.

4. Serve warm.

Per serving: Calories: 155kcal; Fat: 7g; Carbs: 1g; Protein: 22g; Phosphorus: 237mg; Sodium: 53mg; Potassium: 461mg

89. Tuna Casserole

Preparation time: 15 minutes

Cooking time: 35 minutes

Servings: 4

Ingredients:

- ½ cup Cheddar cheese, shredded
- 2 Red bell peppers, chopped
- 7 oz. tuna filet, chopped
- 1 teaspoon ground coriander

- ½ teaspoon salt
- 1 teaspoon olive oil
- ½ teaspoon dried oregano

Directions:

1. Brush the casserole mold with olive oil. Mix up together chopped tuna fillet with dried oregano and ground coriander.

2. Place the fish in the mold and flatten it well to get the layer. Then add chopped Red bell peppers and shredded cheese. Cover the casserole with foil and secure the edges. Bake the meal for 35 minutes at 355F. Serve.

Per serving: Calories: 260kcal; Fat: 22g; Carbs: 3g; Protein: 15g; Phosphorus: 153mg; Sodium: 600mg; Potassium: 311mg

90. Broiled Shrimp

Preparation time: 2 minutes

Cooking time: 5 minutes

Servings: 8

Ingredients:

- 1 lb. shrimp in shell
- 1/2 cup oil, melted
- 2 teaspoons lemon juice
- 2 tablespoons chopped onion
- 1 clove garlic, minced
- 1/8 teaspoon pepper

Directions:

1. Toss the shrimp with the oil, lemon juice, onion, garlic, and pepper in a bowl.

2. Spread the seasoned shrimp in a baking tray.

3. Broil for 5 minutes in an oven on the broiler setting.

4. Serve warm.

Per serving: Calories: 164kcal; Fat: 13g; Carbs: 1g; Protein: 15g; Phosphorus: 215mg; Sodium: 242mg; Potassium: 228mg

91. Sardine Fish Cakes

Preparation time: 10 minutes

Cooking time: 10 minutes

Servings: 4

Ingredients:

- 11 oz. sardines, canned, drained
- 1/3 cup shallot, chopped
- 1 teaspoon chili flakes
- ½ teaspoon salt
- 2 tablespoon wheat flour, whole grain
- 1 egg, beaten
- 1 tablespoon chives, chopped
- 1 teaspoon olive oil
- 1 teaspoon oil

Directions:

1. Put the oil in your skillet and dissolve it. Add shallot and cook it until translucent. After this, transfer the shallot to the mixing bowl.

2. Add sardines, chili flakes, salt, flour, egg, and chives, and mix up until smooth with the fork's help. Make the medium size cakes and place them in the skillet. Add olive oil.

3. Roast the fish cakes for 3 minutes from each side over medium heat. Dry the cooked fish cakes with a paper towel if needed and transfer them to the serving plates.

Per serving: Calories: 221kcal; Fat: 12g; Carbs: 5g; Protein: 21g; Phosphorus: 188mg; Sodium: 453mg; Potassium: 160mg

92. Citrus Glazed Salmon

Preparation time: 5 minutes

Cooking time: 12 minutes

Servings: 4

Ingredients:

- 2 garlic cloves, crushed
- 1 1/2 tablespoons lemon juice
- 2 tablespoons olive oil
- 1 tablespoon oil
- 1 tablespoon Dijon mustard
- 2 dashes cayenne pepper
- 1 teaspoon dried basil leaves
- 1 teaspoon dried dill
- 24 oz. salmon filet

Directions:

1. Place a 1-quart saucepan over moderate heat and add the oil, garlic, lemon juice, mustard, cayenne pepper, dill, and basil to the pan.

2. Stir this mixture for 5 minutes after it has boiled.

3. Prepare and preheat a charcoal grill over moderate heat.

4. Place the fish on a foil sheet, then fold the edges to make a foil tray.

5. Pour the prepared sauce over the fish.

6. Place the fish in the foil on the preheated grill and cook for 12 minutes.

7. Slice and serve.

Per serving: Calories: 401kcal; Fat: 21g; Carbs: 1g; Protein: 49g; Phosphorus: 214mg; Sodium: 256mg; Potassium: 446mg

93. Asparagus Shrimp Linguini

Preparation time: 10 minutes
Cooking time: 35 minutes
Servings: 1 ½ cups
Ingredients:

- 8 ounces of uncooked linguini
- 1 tablespoon of olive oil
- 1¾ cups of asparagus
- ½ cup of unsalted butter
- 2 garlic cloves
- 3 ounces of cream cheese
- 2 tablespoons of fresh parsley
- ¾ teaspoon of dried basil
- 2/3 cup of dry white wine
- ½ pound of peeled and cooked shrimp

Directions:

1. Preheat oven to 350° F
2. Cook the linguini in boiling water 'til it becomes tender, then drain
3. Place the asparagus on a baking sheet, then spread two tablespoons of oil over the asparagus. Bake for about 7 to 8 minutes or until it is tender
4. Remove baked asparagus from the oven and place it on a plate. Cut the asparagus into pieces of medium-sized once cooled
5. Mince the garlic and chop the parsley
6. Melt ½ cup of butter in a large skillet with the minced garlic
7. Stir in the cream cheese, mixing as it melts
8. Stir in the parsley and basil, then simmer for about 5 minutes. Mix either in boiling water or dry white wine, stirring until the sauce becomes smooth
9. Add the cooked shrimp and asparagus, then stir and heat until it is evenly warm
10. Toss the cooked pasta with the sauce and serve

Per serving: Calories: 544kcal; Fat: 32g; Carbs: 43g; Protein: 21g; Phosphorus: 225mg; Sodium: 170mg; Potassium: 402mg

94. Spiced Honey Salmon

Preparation time: 3 minutes
Cooking time: 15 minutes
Servings: 4
Ingredients:

- 3 tablespoons honey
- 3/4 teaspoon lemon peel
- 1/2 teaspoon black pepper
- 1/2 teaspoon garlic powder
- 1 teaspoon water
- 16 oz. salmon fillets
- 2 tablespoons olive oil
- Dill, chopped, to serve

Directions:

1. Whisk the lemon peel with honey, garlic powder, hot water, and ground pepper in a small bowl.
2. Rub this honey mixture over the salmon fillet liberally.
3. Set a suitable skillet over moderate heat and add olive oil to heat.
4. Set the spiced salmon fillets in the pan and sear them for 4 minutes per side.
5. Garnish with dill.

6. Serve warm.

Per serving: Calories: 264kcal; Fat: 14g; Carbs: 14g; Protein: 23g; Phosphorus: 174mg; Sodium: 55mg; Potassium: 507mg

95. Fish En' Papillote

Preparation time: 15 minutes
Cooking time: 20 minutes
Servings: 3
Ingredients:

• 10 oz. snapper fillet
• 1 tablespoon fresh dill, chopped
• 1 white onion, peeled and sliced
• ½ teaspoon tarragon
• 1 tablespoon olive oil
• 1 teaspoon salt
• ½ teaspoon hot pepper
• 2 tablespoons sour cream

Directions:

1. Make the medium size packets from parchment and arrange them in the baking tray. Cut the snapper fillet into three and sprinkle them with salt, tarragon, and hot pepper.

2. Put the fish fillets in the parchment packets. Then top the fish with olive oil, sour cream, sliced onion, and fresh dill. Bake the fish for 20 minutes at 355F. Serve.

Per serving: Calories: 204kcal; Fat: 8g; Carbs: 5g; Protein: 27g; Phosphorus: 139mg; Sodium: 60mg; Potassium: 182mg

Soups

96. Nutmeg Chicken Soup

Preparation time: 10 minutes
Cooking time: 20 minutes
Servings: 4
Ingredients:

• 1 lb. boneless, skinless chicken breasts, uncooked
• 1 1/2 cups onion, sliced
• 1 1/2 cups celery, chopped
• 1 tbsp olive oil
• 1 cup fresh carrots, chopped
• 1 cup fresh green beans, chopped
• 3 tbsp all-purpose white flour
• 1 tsp dried oregano
• 2 tsp dried basil
• 1/4 tsp nutmeg
• 1 tsp thyme
• 32 oz reduced-sodium chicken broth
• 1/2 cup 1% low-fat milk
• 2 cups frozen green peas
• 1/4 tsp black pepper

Directions:

1. Add chicken to a skillet and sauté for 6 minutes, then remove it from the heat.
2. Warm up olive oil in a pan and sauté onion for 5 minutes.
3. Stir in green beans, carrots, chicken, basil, oregano, flour, thyme, and nutmeg.
4. Sauté for 3 minutes, then transfer the ingredients to a large pan.
5. Add milk and broth and cook until it boils.
6. Stir in green peas and cook for 5 minutes.
7. Adjust seasoning with pepper and serve warm.

Per serving: Calories: 131kcal; Fat: 3g; Carbs: 12g; Protein: 14g; Phosphorus: 171mg; Sodium: 343mg; Potassium: 467mg

97. Squash And Turmeric Soup

Preparation time: 10 minutes
Cooking time: 30 minutes
Servings: 4
Ingredients:

• 4 cups low-sodium vegetable broth
• 2 medium zucchini squash, peeled and diced
• 2 medium yellow crookneck squash, peeled and diced
• 1 small onion, diced
• 1/2 cup frozen green peas
• 2 tbsp olive oil
• 1/2 cup plain nonfat Greek yogurt
• 2 tsp turmeric

Directions:

1. Warm the broth in a saucepan on medium heat.
2. Toss in onion, squash, and zucchini.
3. Let it simmer for approximately 25 minutes, then add oil and green peas.
4. Cook for another 5 minutes, then allow it to cool.
5. Puree the soup using a handheld blender, then add Greek yogurt and turmeric.
6. Refrigerate it overnight and serve fresh.

Per serving: Calories: 100kcal; Fat: 5g; Carbs: 10g; Protein: 4g; Phosphorus: 138mg; Sodium: 279mg; Potassium: 504mg

98. Hungarian Cherry Soup

Preparation time: 10 minutes

Cooking time: 15 minutes

Servings: 4

Ingredients:

- 1 1/2 cups fresh cherries
- 3 cups water
- 2 cups stevia
- 1/16 tsp salt
- 1 tbsp all-purpose white flour
- 1/2 cup reduced-fat sour cream

Directions:

1. Warm the water in a saucepan and add cherries and stevia.

2. Let it boil, then simmer for 10 minutes.

3. Remove 2 tbsp of the cooking liquid and keep it aside.

4. Separate ¼ cup of liquid in a bowl and allow it to cool.

5. Add flour and sour cream to this liquid.

6. Mix well, then return the mixture to the saucepan. Cook for 5 minutes on low heat. Garnish the soup with the reserved 2 tbsp of liquid. Serve and enjoy.

Per serving: Calories: 144kcal; Fat: 4g; Carbs: 25g; Protein: 2g; Phosphorus: 40mg; Sodium: 57mg; Potassium: 144mg

99. Cabbage Turkey Soup

Preparation time: 10 minutes

Cooking time: 40-45 minutes

Servings: 1

Ingredients:

- ½ cup shredded green cabbage
- ½ cup bulgur
- 2 dried bay leaves
- 2 tablespoons chopped fresh parsley
- 1 teaspoon chopped fresh sage
- 1 teaspoon chopped fresh thyme
- 1 celery stalk, chopped
- 1 carrot, sliced thin
- ½ sweet onion, chopped
- 1 teaspoon minced garlic
- 1 teaspoon olive oil
- ½ pound cooked ground turkey, 93% lean
- 4 cups water
- 1 cup chicken stock
- Pinch red pepper flakes
- Black pepper (ground), to taste

Directions:

1. Take a large saucepan or cooking pot, and add oil. Heat over medium heat.

2. Add turkey and stir-cook for 4-5 minutes until evenly brown.

3. Add onion and garlic, and sauté for about 3 minutes to soften the veggies.

4. Add water, chicken stock, cabbage, bulgur, celery, carrot, and bay leaves.

5. Boil the mixture.

6. Over low heat, cover and simmer the mixture for about 30-35 minutes until the bulgur is cooked well and tender.

7. Remove bay leaves. Add parsley, sage, thyme, and red pepper flakes; stir the mixture and season with black pepper. Serve warm.

Per serving: Calories: 83kcal; Fat: 4g; Carbs: 2g; Protein: 8g; Phosphorus: 91mg; Sodium: 63mg; Potassium: 185mg

100. Classic Chicken Soup

Preparation time: 5-10 minutes

Cooking time: 35 minutes

Servings: 1

Ingredients:

- 2 teaspoons minced garlic
- 2 celery stalks, chopped
- 1 tablespoon oil
- ½ sweet onion, diced
- 1 carrot, diced
- 4 cups water
- 1 teaspoon chopped fresh thyme
- 2 cups chopped cooked chicken breast
- 1 cup chicken stock
- Black pepper (ground), to taste
- 2 tablespoons chopped fresh parsley

Directions:

1. Take a medium-large cooking pot and heat oil over medium heat.

2. Add onion and stir-cook until it becomes translucent and softened.

3. Add garlic and stir-cook until it becomes fragrant.

4. Add celery, carrot, chicken, chicken stock, and water. Boil the mixture.

5. Over low heat, simmers the mixture for about 25-30 minutes until the veggies are tender.

6. Mix in thyme and cook for 2 minutes. Season to taste with black pepper.

7. Serve warm with parsley on top.

Per serving: Calories: 135kcal; Fat: 6g; Carbs: 3g; Protein: 15g; Phosphorus: 122mg; Sodium: 74mg; Potassium: 208mg

101. Green Bean Veggie Stew

Preparation time: 10 minutes

Cooking time: 30-35 minutes

Servings: 1

Ingredients:

- 6 cups shredded green cabbage
- 3 celery stalks, chopped
- 1 teaspoon oil
- ½ large sweet onion, chopped
- 1 teaspoon minced garlic
- 1 scallion, chopped
- 2 tablespoons chopped fresh parsley
- 2 tablespoons lemon juice
- 1 teaspoon chopped fresh oregano
- 1 tablespoon chopped fresh thyme
- 1 teaspoon chopped savory
- Water
- 1 cup fresh green beans, cut into 1" pieces
- Black pepper (ground), to taste

Directions:

1. Take a medium-large cooking pot and heat oil over medium heat.

2. Add onion and stir-cook until it becomes translucent and soft.

3. Add garlic and stir-cook until it becomes fragrant.

4. Add cabbage, celery, scallion, parsley, lemon juice, thyme, savory, and oregano; add water to cover veggies by 3-4 inches.

5. Stir the mixture and boil it.

6. Over low heat, cover and simmer the mixture for about 25 minutes until the veggies are tender.

7. Add green beans and cook for 2-3 more minutes. Season with black pepper to taste. Serve warm.

Per serving: Calories: 56kcal; Fat: 1g; Carbs: 7g; Protein: 1g; Phosphorus: 194mg; Sodium: 31mg; Potassium: 194mg

102. Mediterranean Vegetable Soup

Preparation time: 5 minutes

Cooking time: 30 minutes

Servings: 4

Ingredients:

- 1 tbsp. oregano
- 2 minced garlic cloves
- 1 tsp. black pepper
- 1 diced zucchini
- 1 cup diced eggplant
- 4 cups water
- 1 diced red pepper
- 1 tbsp. extra-virgin olive oil
- 1 diced red onion

Directions:

1. Soak the vegetables in warm water before use.

2. Add the oil, chopped onion, and minced garlic to a large pot.

3. Simmer for 5 minutes on low heat.

4. Add the other vegetables to the onions and cook for 7-8 minutes.

5. Add the stock to the pan and bring it to a boil on high heat.

6. Stir in the herbs, reduce the heat, and simmer for 20 minutes or until thoroughly cooked.

7. Season with pepper to serve.

Per serving: Calories: 152kcal; Fat: 3g; Carbs: 6g; Protein: 1g; Phosphorus: 45mg; Sodium: 3mg; Potassium: 229mg

103. Oxtail Soup

Preparation time: 10 minutes

Cooking time: 20 minutes

Servings: 4

Ingredients:

- 1 medium bell pepper, diced
- 1 small jalapeno pepper, diced
- 1 large onion, sliced
- 3 celery stalks, chopped
- 1 tbsp olive oil
- 1 tbsp all-purpose white flour
- 2 bouillon cubes
- 2-lb package oxtail
- 1 tbsp vinegar
- 1/4 tsp black pepper
- 1/2 tsp herb seasoning blend
- 12 oz frozen gumbo vegetables

Directions:

1. Add olive oil, flour, and bouillon cubes to a saucepan.

2. Add water 3/4 of the way up the saucepan and let it boil.

3. Stir in peppers, vinegar, and oxtails.

4. Cover it and cook until the oxtails soften.

5. Add all vegetables, including celery and onion, to the soup.

6. Cook until the veggies soften.

7. Serve fresh and warm.

Per serving: Calories: 313kcal; Fat: 21g; Carbs: 10g; Protein: 21g; Phosphorus: 257mg; Sodium: 325mg; Potassium: 596mg

104. Turkey & Lemon-Grass Soup

Preparation time: 5 minutes

Cooking time: 40 minutes

Servings: 4

Ingredients:

- 1 fresh lime
- ¼ cup fresh basil leaves
- 1 tbsp. cilantro
- 1 cup chestnuts
- 1 tbsp. coconut oil
- 1 thumb-size minced ginger piece
- 2 chopped scallions
- 1 finely chopped green chili
- 4oz. skinless and sliced turkey breasts
- 1 minced garlic clove, minced
- ½ finely sliced stick of lemon-grass
- 1 chopped white onion, chopped
- 4 cups water

Directions:

1. Crush the lemon grass, cilantro, chili, 1 tbsp oil and basil leaves in a blender or pestle and mortar to form a paste.

2. Heat a large pan/wok with 1 tbsp olive oil.

3. Sauté the onions, garlic and ginger until soft.

4. Add the turkey and brown each side for 4-5 minutes.

5. Add the broth and stir.

6. Now add the paste and stir.

7. Next, add the chestnuts, cool the heat slightly, and simmer for 25-30 minutes or until the turkey is thoroughly cooked.

8. Serve hot with the green onion sprinkled over the top.

Per serving: Calories: 123kcal; Fat: 3g; Carbs: 12g; Protein: 10g; Phosphorus: 110mg; Sodium: 501mg; Potassium: 151mg

105. Eggplant And Red Pepper Soup

Preparation time: 20 minutes

Cooking time: 40 minutes

Servings: 6

Ingredients:

- Sweet onion – 1 small, cut into quarters
- Small red bell peppers – 2, halved
- Cubed eggplant – 2 cups
- Garlic – 2 cloves, crushed
- Olive oil – 1 Tbsp.
- Chicken stock – 1 cup
- Water
- Chopped fresh basil – ¼ cup
- Ground black pepper

Directions:

1. Preheat the oven to 350F.

2. Put the onions, red peppers, eggplant, and garlic in a baking dish.

3. Drizzle the vegetables with olive oil.

4. Roast the vegetables for 30 minutes until they are slightly charred and soft.

5. Cool the vegetables slightly and remove the skin from the peppers.

6. Puree the vegetables with a hand mixer (with the chicken stock).

7. Transfer the soup to a medium pot and add enough water to reach the desired thickness.

8. Heat the soup to a simmer and add the basil.

9. Season with pepper and serve.

Per serving: Calories: 61kcal; Fat: 2g; Carbs: 9g; Protein: 2g; Phosphorus: 122mg; Sodium: 98mg; Potassium: 342mg

106. Wild Rice Asparagus Soup

Preparation time: 10 minutes

Cooking time: 30 minutes

Servings: 4

Ingredients:

- 3/4 cup wild rice
- 2 cups asparagus, chopped
- 1 cup carrots, diced
- 1/2 cup onion, diced
- 3 garlic cloves, minced
- 1/4 cup oil
- 1/2 tsp thyme
- 1/2 tsp fresh ground pepper
- 1/4 tsp nutmeg
- 1 bay leaf
- 1/2 cup all-purpose flour
- 4 cups low-sodium chicken broth

- 1/2 cup extra dry vermouth
- 2 cups cooked chicken
- 4 cups unsweetened almond milk, unenriched

Directions:

1. Cook the wild rice as per the cooking instructions on the box or bag and drain.

2. Melt the oil in a Dutch oven and sauté garlic and onion.

3. Once soft, add spices, herbs, and carrots.

4. Cook on medium heat until veggies are tender, then add flour and stir; cook for 10 minutes on low heat.

5. Add 4 cups of broth and vermouth and blend using a handheld blender.

6. Dice the chicken pieces and add asparagus and chicken to the soup.

7. Stir in almond milk and cook for 20 minutes.

8. Add the wild rice and serve warm.

Per serving: Calories: 295kcal; Fat: 11g; Carbs: 28g; Protein: 21g; Phosphorus: 252mg; Sodium: 385mg; Potassium: 527mg

107. Paprika Pork Soup

Preparation time: 5 minutes

Cooking time: 35 minutes

Servings: 2

Ingredients:

- 4-ounce sliced pork loin
- 1 teaspoon black pepper
- 2 minced garlic cloves
- 3 cups water
- 1 tablespoon extra-virgin olive oil
- 1 chopped onion

- 1 tablespoon paprika

Directions:

1. Add in the oil, chopped onion and minced garlic.

2. Sauté for 5 minutes on low heat.

3. Add the pork slices to the onions and cook for 7-8 minutes or until browned.

4. Add the water to the pan and bring to a boil on high heat.

5. Reduce heat and simmer for 20 minutes or until pork is thoroughly cooked.

6. Season with pepper to serve.

Per serving: Calories: 165kcal; Fat: 9g; Carbs: 10g; Protein: 13g; Phosphorus: 158mg; Sodium: 269mg; Potassium: 486mg

108. Chicken Wild Rice Soup

Preparation time: 10 minutes
Cooking time: 15 minutes
Servings: 6
Ingredients:

- 2/3 cup wild rice, uncooked
- 1 tbsp onion, chopped finely
- 1 tbsp fresh parsley, chopped
- 1 cup carrots, chopped
- 8 oz chicken breast, cooked
- 2 tbsp oil
- 1/4 cup all-purpose white flour
- 5 cups low-sodium chicken broth
- 1 tbsp slivered almonds

Directions:

1. Start by adding rice and 2 cups broth, and ½ cup water to a cooking pot.

2. Cook 'til the rice is al dente and set it aside.

3. Add oil to a saucepan and melt it.

4. Stir in onion and sauté until soft, then add the flour and the remaining broth.

5. Stir and cook for 1 minute, then add the chicken, cooked rice, and carrots.

6. Cook for 5 minutes on simmer.

7. Garnish with almonds. Serve fresh.

Per serving: Calories: 287kcal; Fat: 7g; Carbs: 35g; Protein: 21g; Phosphorus: 217mg; Sodium: 182mg; Potassium: 384mg

109. Beef Okra Soup

Preparation time: 10 minutes
Cooking time: 45-55 minutes
Servings: 1
Ingredients:

- ½ cup okra
- ½ teaspoon basil
- ½ cup carrots, diced
- 3 ½ cups water
- 1-pound beef stew meat
- 1 cup raw sliced onions
- ½ cup green peas
- 1 teaspoon black pepper
- ½ teaspoon thyme
- ½ cup corn kernels

Directions:

1. Take a medium-large cooking pot and heat oil over medium heat.

2. Add water, beef stew meat, black pepper, onions, basil, thyme, and stir-cook for 40-45 minutes until meat is tender.

3. Add all veggies. Over low heat, simmer the mixture for about 20-25 minutes. Add more water if needed.

4. Serve soup warm.

Per serving: Calories: 187kcal; Fat: 12g; Carbs: 7g; Protein: 11g; Phosphorus: 119mg; Sodium: 59mg; Potassium: 288mg

110. Spicy Chicken Soup

Preparation time: 10 minutes

Cooking time: 5 minutes

Servings: 4

Ingredients:

• 2 cups cooked chicken, shredded

• 1/2 cup half and half

• 4 cups chicken broth

• 1/3 cup hot sauce

• 3 tbsp. butter

• 4 oz. cream cheese

• Pepper

• Salt

Directions:

1. Add half and half, broth, hot sauce, butter, and cream cheese into the blender and blend until smooth.

2. Pour the blended mixture into the saucepan and cook over medium heat until hot.

3. Add chicken and stir well. Season soup with pepper and salt.

4. Serve and enjoy.

Per serving: Calories: 361kcal; Fat: 26g; Carbs: 4g; Protein: 28g; Phosphorus: 110mg; Sodium: 75mg; Potassium: 117mg

Snacks

111. Marinated Berries

Preparation time: 5 minutes
Cooking time: 30 minutes
Servings: 4
Ingredients:

- 2 cups fresh strawberries, hulled and quartered
- 1 cup fresh blueberries (optional)
- 2 tablespoons sugar
- 1 tablespoon balsamic vinegar
- 2 tablespoons chopped fresh mint (optional)
- 1/8 teaspoon freshly ground black pepper

Directions:

1. Gently toss the strawberries, blueberries (if using), sugar, vinegar, mint (if using), and pepper in a large nonreactive bowl.

2. Let the flavors blend for at least 25 minutes or as long as 2 hours.

Per serving: Calories: 73kcal; Fat: 8g; Carbs: 18g; Protein: 1g; Phosphorus: 132mg; Sodium: 4mg; Potassium: 162mg

112. Happy Heart Energy Bites

Preparation time: 20 minutes
Cooking time: 30 min
Servings: Makes 30 (2 balls per serving)
Ingredients:

- 1 cup rolled oats
- ¾ cup chopped walnuts
- ½ cup natural peanut butter
- ½ cup ground flaxseed
- ¼ cup honey
- ¼ cup dried cranberries

Directions:

1. In a large bowl, combine the oats, walnuts, peanut butter, flaxseed, honey, and cranberries. Refrigerate for 10 to 20 minutes, if you can, to make them easier to roll.

2. Roll into ¾-inch balls. Store in the fridge or freezer if they don't disappear first.

Per serving: Calories: 174kcal; Fat: 10g; Carbs: 17g; Protein: 5g; Phosphorus: 152mg; Sodium: 43mg; Potassium: 169mg

113. Veggie Snack

Preparation time: 5 minutes
Cooking time: 10 minutes
Servings: 1
Ingredients:

- 1 large yellow pepper
- 5 carrots
- 5 stalks celery

Directions:

1. Clean the carrots and rinse them under running water.

2. Rinse celery and yellow pepper. Remove the seeds of pepper and chop the veggies into small sticks.

3. Put in a bowl and serve.

Per serving: Calories: 189kcal; Fat: 1g; Carbs: 44g; Protein: 5g; Phosphorus: 0mg; Sodium: 282mg; Potassium: 0mg

114. Jalapeno Salsa

Preparation time: 10 minutes

Cooking time: 0 minutes

Servings: 8

Ingredients:

- 4 Roma tomatoes, chopped
- 2 green onions, chopped
- 3 garlic cloves, minced
- 1 green bell pepper, chopped
- 1 fresh jalapeño, chopped
- ½ bunch of fresh cilantro, chopped
- ½ teaspoon cumin
- ¼ cup fresh oregano, chopped

Directions:

1. Add bell pepper, jalapeno, cilantro, tomatoes, onion, and all other ingredients to a blender.

2. Blend this salsa mixture until it gets chunky.

3. Serve fresh.

Per serving: Calories: 14kcal; Fat: 1g; Carbs: 2g; Protein: 1g; Phosphorus: 14mg; Sodium: 4mg; Potassium: 117mg

115. Spicy Crab Dip

Preparation time: 10 minutes

Cooking time: 20 minutes

Servings: 1

Ingredients:

- 1 can of 8 oz. softened cream cheese
- 1 tbsp. finely chopped onions
- 1 tbsp. lemon juice
- 2 tbsp. Worcestershire sauce
- 1/8 tsp. black pepper Cayenne pepper to taste
- 2 tbsp. to s. of almond milk or non-fortified rice drink
- 1 can of 6 oz. of crabmeat

Directions:

1. Preheat the oven to 375 degrees F.

2. Pour the cheese cream into a bowl. Add the onions, lemon juice, Worcestershire sauce, black pepper, and cayenne pepper. Mix well. Stir in the almond milk/rice drink.

3. Add the crabmeat and mix until you obtain a homogeneous mixture.

4. Pour the mixture into a baking dish. Cook without covering for 15 minutes or until bubbles appear. Serve hot with triangle-cut pita bread.

5. Microwave until bubbles appear, about 4 minutes, stirring every 1 to 2 minutes.

Per serving: Calories: 42kcal; Fat: 1g; Carbs: 2g; Protein: 7g; Phosphorus: 139mg; Sodium: 167mg; Potassium: 130mg

116. Addictive Pretzels

Preparation time: 10 minutes

Cooking time: 1 hour

Servings: 6

Ingredients:

- 32-ounce bag of unsalted pretzels
- 1 cup canola oil
- 2 tablespoon seasoning mix
- 3 teaspoon garlic powder
- 3 teaspoons dried dill weed

Directions:

1. Preheat oven to 175 degrees f.

2. Place the pretzels on a cooking sheet and break them into pieces.

3. Mix garlic powder and dill in a bowl and reserve half of the mixture.

4. Mix the remaining half with seasoning mix and ¾ cup of canola oil.

5. Pour this oil over the pretzels and brush them liberally

6. Bake the pieces for 1 hour, then flip them to bake for another 15 minutes.

7. Allow them to cool, then sprinkle the remaining dill mixture and drizzle more oil on top.

8. Serve fresh and warm.

Per serving: Calories: 184kcal; Fat: 8g; Carbs: 22g; Protein: 2g; Phosphorus: 28mg; Sodium: 60mg; Potassium: 43mg

117. Shrimp Spread With Crackers

Preparation time: 10 minutes
Cooking time: 0 minutes
Servings: 6
Ingredients:

- 1/4 cup light cream cheese
- 2 1/2-ounce cooked, shelled shrimp, minced
- 1 tablespoon of no-salt-added ketchup
- 1/4 teaspoon hot sauce
- 1 teaspoon Worcestershire sauce
- 1/2 teaspoon herb seasoning blend
- 24 matzo cracker miniatures
- 1 tablespoon parsley

Directions:

1. Start by tossing the minced shrimp with cream cheese in a bowl.

2. Stir in Worcestershire sauce, hot sauce, herb seasoning, and ketchup.

3. Mix well and garnish with minced parsley.

4. Serve the spread with the crackers.

Per serving: Calories: 57kcal; Fat: 1g; Carbs: 7g; Protein: 3g; Phosphorus: 30mg; Sodium: 69mg; Potassium: 54mg

118. Sweet And Spicy Tortilla Chips

Preparation time: 10 minutes
Cooking time: 8 minutes
Servings: 6
Ingredients:

- 1/4 cup butter
- 1 teaspoon brown sugar
- 1/2 teaspoon ground chili powder
- 1/2 teaspoon garlic powder
- 1/2 teaspoon ground cumin
- 1/4 teaspoon ground cayenne pepper
- 6 flour tortillas, 6" size

Directions:

1. Preheat oven to 425 degrees f.

2. Grease a baking sheet with cooking spray.

3. Add all spices, brown sugar, and melted butter to a small bowl.

4. Mix well and set this mixture aside.

5. Slice the tortillas into eight wedges and brush them with the sugar mixture.

6. Spread them on the baking sheet and bake them for 8 minutes.

7. Serve fresh.

Per serving: Calories: 115kcal; Fat: 7g; Carbs: 11g; Protein: 2g; Phosphorus: 44mg; Sodium: 156mg; Potassium: 42mg

119. Buffalo Chicken Dip

Preparation time: 10 minutes
Cooking time: 3 hours
Servings: 4
Ingredients:

- 4-ounce cream cheese
- 1/2 cup bottled roasted red peppers
- 1 cup reduced-fat sour cream
- 4 teaspoons hot pepper sauce
- 2 cups cooked, shredded chicken

Directions:

1. Blend half a cup of drained red peppers in a food processor until smooth.

2. Now, thoroughly mix cream cheese and sour cream with the pureed peppers in a bowl.

3. Stir in shredded chicken and hot sauce, then transfer the mixture to a slow cooker.

4. Cook for 3 hours on low heat.

5. Serve warm with celery, carrots, cauliflower, and cucumber.

Per serving: Calories: 73kcal; Fat: 5g; Carbs: 2g; Protein: 5g; Phosphorus: 47mg; Sodium: 66mg; Potassium: 81mg

120. Mango Chiller

Preparation time: 5 minutes
Cooking time: 5 minutes
Servings: 4 (½ cup per serving)
Ingredients:

- 2 cups frozen mango chunks
- ½ cup plain 2% Greek yogurt
- ¼ cup 1% almond milk
- 2 teaspoons honey (optional)

Directions:

1. Mix the mango and yogurt in a food processor or blender. Add the almond milk, a bit at a time, to get it to soft ice cream consistency.

2. Taste, and add honey if you like. Enjoy immediately.

Per serving: Calories: 85kcal; Fat: 1g; Carbs: 16g; Protein: 4g; Phosphorus: 112mg; Sodium: 17mg; Potassium: 197mg

121. Vegetable Rolls

Preparation time: 30 minutes
Cooking time: 0 minutes
Servings: 8
Ingredients:

- Finely shredded red cabbage – ½ cup
- Grated carrot – ½ cup
- Julienne red bell pepper – ¼ cup
- Julienned scallion – ¼ cup, both green and white parts
- Chopped cilantro – ¼ cup
- Olive oil – 1 Tablespoon.
- Ground cumin – ¼ teaspoon.
- Freshly ground black pepper – ¼ teaspoon.
- English cucumber – 1, sliced very thin strips

Directions:

1. In a bowl, toss the black pepper, cumin, olive oil, cilantro, scallion, red pepper, carrot, and cabbage. Mix well.

2. Evenly divide the vegetable filling among the cucumber strips, placing the filling close to one end of the strip.

3. Roll up the cucumber strips around the filling and secure them with a wooden pick.

4. Repeat with each cucumber strip.

Per serving: Calories: 26kcal; Fat: 2g; Carbs: 3g; Protein: 0g; Phosphorus: 14mg; Sodium: 7mg; Potassium: 7mg

122. Baba Ghanouj

Preparation time: 10 minutes

Cooking time: 1 hour and 20 minutes

Servings: 1

Ingredients:

• 1 large aubergine, cut in half lengthwise

• 1 head of garlic, unpeeled

• 30 ml (2 tablespoons) of olive oil

• Lemon juice to taste

Directions:

1. Preheat the oven to 350 degrees F.

2. Place the eggplant on the plate, skin side up. Roast until the meat is tender and detaches easily from the skin, about 1 hour, depending on the eggplant's size. Let cool.

3. Meanwhile, cut the tip of the garlic cloves. Put garlic cloves in a square of aluminum foil. Fold the edges of the sheet and fold them together to form a tightly wrapped foil.

4. Roast with the eggplant until tender, about 20 minutes. Let cool. Purée the pods with a garlic press.

5. With a spoon, scoop out the eggplant's flesh and place it in the bowl of a food processor. Add the garlic puree, the oil, and the lemon juice. Stir until purée is smooth and pepper.

6. Serve with mini pita bread.

Per serving: Calories: 110kcal; Fat: 12g; Carbs: 5g; Protein: 1g; Phosphorus: 81mg; Sodium: 180mg; Potassium: 207mg

123. Pecan Caramel Corn

Preparation time: 10 minutes

Cooking time: 1 hour, 5 minutes

Servings: 10

Ingredients:

• 20 cups popped popcorn

• 2 cups unbranched almonds

• 1 cup pecan halves

• 2 cups stevia

• 1 cup oil

• ½ cup corn syrup

• Pinch cream of tartar

• 1 teaspoon baking soda

Directions:

1. Layer a large roasting pan with popcorn, almonds, and pecans.

2. Cook stevia with corn syrup, oil, and cream of tartar in a heavy saucepan.

3. Stir this syrup for 5 minutes on a boil, then stir in baking soda.

4. Pour this caramel sauce over the popcorn and almonds in the pan.

5. Bake the almonds and popcorn for 1 hour at 200°F in the oven.

6. Stir well, then serve.

Per serving: Calories: 604kcal; Fat: 6g; Carbs: 51g; Protein: 8g; Phosphorus: 201mg; Sodium: 149mg; Potassium: 285mg

124. Sautéed Spicy Cabbage

Preparation time: 15 minutes

Cooking time: 5 minutes

Servings: 6

Ingredients:

• 3 tablespoons olive oil

• 3 cups chopped green cabbage

• 3 cups chopped red cabbage

• 2 garlic cloves, minced

• 1/8 teaspoon cayenne pepper

• Pinch salt

Direction

1. Cook olive oil in a large skillet over medium heat.

2. Stir in red and green cabbage and the garlic; sauté until the leaves wilt and are tender, about 4 to 5 minutes.

3. Sprinkle the vegetables with the cayenne pepper and salt, toss, and serve.

Per serving: Calories: 86kcal; Fat: 6g; Carbs: 23g; Protein: 1g; Phosphorus: 27mg; Sodium: 46mg; Potassium: 189mg

125. Roasted Asparagus With Pine Nuts

Preparation time: 10 minutes

Cooking time: 13 minutes

Servings: 4

Ingredients:

• 1-pound fresh asparagus, woody ends removed

• 1 tablespoon olive oil

• 1 tablespoon balsamic vinegar

• 3 garlic cloves, minced

• ½ teaspoon dried thyme leaves

• ¼ cup pine nuts

Direction

1. Preheat the oven to 400°F.

2. Rinse the asparagus and arrange it in a single layer on a baking sheet.

3. Blend olive oil, balsamic vinegar, garlic, and thyme until well-mixed.

4. Drizzle the dressing over the asparagus and toss to coat.

5. Roast the asparagus for 10 minutes and remove the baking sheet from the oven.

6. Sprinkle the pine nuts over the asparagus and return the baking sheet to the oven. Roast for another 5 to 7 minutes or until the pine nuts are toasted and the asparagus is tender and light golden brown. Serve.

Per serving: Calories: 116kcal; Fat: 6g; Carbs: 23g; Protein: 4g; Phosphorus: 112mg; Sodium: 4mg; Potassium: 294mg

126. Popcorn With Sugar And Spice

Preparation time: 10 minutes

Cooking time: 10 minutes

Servings: 2

Ingredients:

• 8 cups hot popcorn

• 2 tablespoons unsalted butter

• 2 tablespoons sugar

• 1/2 teaspoon cinnamon

• 1/4 teaspoon nutmeg

Directions:

1. Popping the corn, put aside.

2. Heat the butter, sugar, cinnamon, and nutmeg in the microwave or saucepan over a range fire 'til the butter is melted, and the sugar dissolves.

3. Sprinkle the corn with the spicy butter, and mix well.

4. Serve immediately for optimal flavor.

Per serving: Calories: 120kcal; Fat: 7g; Carbs: 12g; Protein: 2g; Phosphorus: 60mg; Sodium: 2mg; Potassium: 56mg

127. Rosemary And White Bean Dip

Preparation time: 10 minutes

Cooking time: 10 minutes

Servings: 10 (¼ cup per serving)

Ingredients:

• 1 (15-ounce) can of cannellini beans, rinsed and drained

• 2 tablespoons extra-virgin olive oil

• 1 garlic clove, peeled

• 1 teaspoon finely chopped fresh rosemary

• Pinch cayenne pepper

• Freshly ground black pepper

• 1 (7.5-ounce) jar marinated artichoke hearts, drained

Directions:

1. Blend the beans, oil, garlic, rosemary, cayenne pepper, and black pepper in a food processor until smooth.

2. Add the artichoke hearts, and pulse until roughly chopped but not puréed.

Per serving: Calories: 75kcal; Fat: 5g; Carbs: 6g; Protein: 2g; Phosphorus: 128mg; Sodium: 139mg; Potassium: 75mg

128. Blueberry-Ricotta Swirl

Preparation time: 5 minutes

Cooking time: 5 minutes

Servings: 2

Ingredients:

• ½ cup fresh or frozen blueberries

• ½ cup part-skim ricotta cheese

• 1 teaspoon sugar

• ½ teaspoon lemon zest (optional)

Directions:

1. If using frozen blueberries, warm them in a saucepan over medium heat until they are thawed but not hot.

2. Meanwhile, mix the sugar with the ricotta in a medium bowl.

3. Mix the blueberries into the ricotta, leaving a few out. Taste, and add more sugar if desired. Top with the remaining blueberries and lemon zest (if using).

Per serving: Calories: 113kcal; Fat: 5g; Carbs: 10g; Protein: 7g; Phosphorus: 102mg; Sodium: 62mg; Potassium: 98mg

129. Spicy Guacamole

Preparation time: 15 minutes

Cooking time: 15 minutes

Servings: 4 (about three tablespoons per serving)

Ingredients:

• 1½ tablespoons freshly squeezed lime juice

• 1 tablespoon minced jalapeño pepper, or to taste

• 1 tablespoon minced red onion

- 1 tablespoon chopped fresh cilantro
- 1 garlic clove, minced
- 1/8 to ¼ teaspoon kosher salt
- Freshly ground black pepper

Directions:

1. Mix well with the lime juice, jalapeño, onion, cilantro, garlic, salt, and pepper in a large bowl.

Per serving: Calories: 61kcal; Fat: 5g; Carbs: 4g; Protein: 16g; Phosphorus: 154mg; Sodium: 123mg; Potassium: 195mg

130. Roasted Radishes

Preparation time: 10 minutes

Cooking time: 20 minutes

Servings: 6

Ingredients:

- 3 bunches of whole small radishes
- 3 tablespoons olive oil, divided
- 1 tablespoon freshly squeezed lemon juice
- 1 tablespoon Dijon mustard
- ½ teaspoon dried marjoram leaves
- 1/8 teaspoon white pepper
- Pinch salt
- 2 tablespoons chopped flat-leaf parsley

Direction

1. Preheat the oven to 425°F. Prep a baking sheet with a lip with parchment paper and set aside.

2. Scrub the radishes, remove the stem and root, and cut each in half or thirds, depending on the size. The radishes should be similarly sized so they cook evenly.

3. Toss the radishes and one tablespoon of olive oil on the baking sheet to coat and arrange the radishes in a single layer.

4. Roast the radishes for 18 to 20 minutes or until they are slightly golden and tender but crisp outside.

5. While the radishes are roasting, whisk together the remaining two tablespoons of olive oil with the lemon juice, mustard, marjoram, pepper, and salt in a small bowl.

6. Once done, take them from the baking sheet and place them in a serving bowl. Drizzle the vegetables with the dressing and toss. Sprinkle with parsley. Serve warm or cool.

Per serving: Calories: 79kcal; Fat: 4g; Carbs: 8g; Protein: 1g; Phosphorus: 23mg; Sodium: 123mg; Potassium: 232mg

Desserts

131. Small Chocolate Cakes

Preparation time: 15 minutes

Cooking time: 1 minute

Servings: 2

Ingredients:

• 1 box of angel food cake mix

• 1 box lemon cake mix

• water

• nonstick cooking spray or batter

• dark chocolate small squared chops and chocolate powder

Directions:

1. Use a transparent kitchen cooking bag and put inside both lemon cake mixes, angel food mixes, and chocolate squared chops. Mix everything and put water to prepare a small cupcake.

2. Put the mix in a mold to prepare a cupcake containing the ingredients and put it in the microwave for a one-minute high temperature.

3. Slip the cupcake out of the mold, put it on a dish, let it cool, and put some more chocolate crumbs on it. Serve and enjoy!

Per serving: Calories: 95kcal; Fat: 3g; Carbs: 28g; Protein: 1g; Phosphorus: 80mg; Sodium: 162mg; Potassium: 15mg

132. Strawberry Tiramisu

Preparation time: 15 minutes

Cooking time: 10 minutes

Servings: 4

Ingredients:

• 4 ladyfingers

• 4 tbsp almond syrup or amaretto

• 1 cup stevia

• 1/2 vanilla pod

• 100g mascarpone

• 200g cream quark

• 1 tbsp chopped pistachios

• 200g strawberries

Directions:

1. Puree half of the strawberries with one tablespoon of stevia and the vanilla pulp. Cut the remaining strawberries into small pieces. Mix the mascarpone and cream quark with the remaining stevia.

2. Break the sponge fingers into pieces and divide them into four glasses. Pour almond syrup over it, then spread the strawberry puree and strawberries on top. Pour in the quark mixture and garnish with a piece of strawberry and pistachios.

3. Let soak in the refrigerator for an hour.

Per serving: Calories: 315kcal; Fat: 21g; Carbs: 24g; Protein: 7g; Phosphorus: 154mg; Sodium: 89mg; Potassium: 185mg

133. Chocolate Beet Cake

Preparation time: 15 minutes

Cooking time: 50 minutes

Servings: 12

Ingredients:

• 3 cups grated beets

• 1/4 cup canola oil

- 4 eggs
- 4 oz. unsweetened chocolate
- 2 tsp. phosphorus-free baking powder
- 2 cups all-purpose flour
- 1 cup stevia

Directions:

1. Set your oven to 325 F. Grease two 8-inch cake pans. Mix the baking powder, flour, and stevia. Set aside.

2. Chop the chocolate and dissolve it using a double boiler. A microwave can also be used, but don't let it burn.

3. Allow it to cool, and then mix in the oil and eggs. Mix all the wet fixings into the flour mixture until well-mixed.

4. Fold the beets in and pour the batter into the cake pans. Let them bake for 40 to 50 minutes. To know it's done, the toothpick should come out clean when inserted into the cake.

5. Remove, then allow them to cool. Once cool, invert over a plate to remove. It is great when served with whipped cream and fresh berries. Enjoy!

Per serving: Calories: 270kcal; Fat: 17g; Carbs: 31g; Protein: 6g; Phosphorus: 111mg; Sodium: 109mg; Potassium: 299mg

134. Chocolate Pie Shell

Preparation time: 15 minutes
Cooking time: 0 minutes
Servings: 6
Ingredients:

- 3 cups cocoa krispies, crushed
- 4 tablespoon oil, ½ stick
- cooking spray

Directions:

1. Crush the cocoa Krispies, melt the oil, add both to a bowl, and stir. Oiled a 9-inch pie pan using cooking spray, then pressed the mixture into the pie pan.

2. Place in the refrigerator to chill for a minimum of 30 minutes before filling. You can add any filling of your choice

Per serving: Calories: 126kcal; Fat: 0g; Carbs: 18g; Protein: 2g; Phosphorus: 24mg; Sodium: 135mg; Potassium: 47mg

135. Fruit Salad

Preparation time: 15 minutes
Cooking time: 0 minutes
Servings: 10
Ingredients:

- 1 cup canned pineapple chunks, drained
- 2 cups canned fruit cocktail, drained
- 1 cup sliced or whole strawberries hulled
- 1 cup marshmallows
- 1 cup peeled, cored, and chopped apple
- 1/2 cup non-dairy whipped topping

Directions:

1. Mix all the fruits in a bowl. Add the whipped topping and marshmallows. Mix well. Refrigerate for at least an hour. Serve chilled!

Per serving: Calories: 57kcal; Fat: 0g; Carbs: 14g; Protein: 1g; Phosphorus: 15mg; Sodium: 9mg; Potassium: 120mg

136. Fruit Crunch

Preparation time: 15 minutes

Cooking time: 35 minutes

Servings: 8

Ingredients:

- 4 tart apples, pare, core and slice
- 2 cup stevia
- 1/2 cup sifted all-purpose flour
- 1/3 cup margarine, softened
- 3/4 cup rolled oats
- 3/4 tsp nutmeg

Directions:

1. Preheat your oven to 375 degrees. Place the apples in a greased square 8-inch pan. Mix the other ingredients in a medium-sized bowl and spread the mixture over the apple. Bake within 35 minutes or until the Apple turns lightly brown and tender.

Per serving: Calories: 217kcal; Fat: 6g; Carbs: 36g; Protein: 2g; Phosphorus: 37mg; Sodium: 62mg; Potassium: 68mg

137. Chocolate Muffins

Preparation time: 10 minutes

Cooking time: 30 minutes

Servings: 10

Ingredients:

- 2 eggs, lightly beaten
- 1/2 cup cream
- 1/2 tsp vanilla
- 1 cup almond flour
- 1 tbsp baking powder, gluten-free
- 4 tbsp Swerve
- 1/2 cup unsweetened cocoa powder
- Pinch of salt

Directions:

1. Preheat the oven to 375 F.

2. Spray a muffin tray with cooking spray and then set aside.

3. Mix almond flour, baking powder, swerve, cocoa powder, and salt in a mixing bowl.

4. In a different bowl, beat eggs with cream and vanilla.

5. Place the egg mixture into the almond flour mixture and mix well.

6. Pour batter into the prepared muffin tray, then bake in preheated oven for 30 minutes.

7. Serve and enjoy.

Per serving: Calories: 101kcal; Fat: 8g; Carbs: 7g; Protein: 5g; Phosphorus: 75mg; Sodium: 78mg; Potassium: 57mg

138. Jeweled Cookies

Preparation time: 15 minutes

Cooking time: 10 minutes

Servings: 50 cookies

Ingredients:

- 1/2 cup softened unsalted margarine or oil
- 1 3/4 cups sifted all-purpose flour
- 2 cup stevia
- 1 medium egg
- 1 tsp vanilla
- 1/4 cup milk
- 1 tsp baking powder
- 15 large gumdrops

Directions:

1. Preheat your oven to 400 degrees. Mix the egg, oil, and stevia thoroughly in a bowl. Add in vanilla and milk, then stir.

2. Mix the flour and baking powder in a different bowl. Add to the previous mixture. Now add the gumdrops and stir, then chill for a minimum of one hour.

3. Spoon the dough using a tablespoon, then put it on an oiled cookie sheet. Bake for approximately 10 minutes or until it turns golden brown.

Per serving: Calories: 104kcal; Fat: 6g; Carbs: 22g; Protein: 1g; Phosphorus: 16mg; Sodium: 9mg; Potassium: 29mg

139. Whipped Cream Pound Cake

Preparation time: 15 minutes

Cooking time: 60 minutes

Servings: 30 slices

Ingredients:

• 2 sticks of oil or margarine, softened

• 6 eggs

• 6 cups stevia

• 1/2-pint whipping cream

• 3 cups cake flour, sift once before you measure

• 1 tsp vanilla flavoring

Directions:

1. Preheat your oven to 350 degrees. Oil and flour in a tube/ baking pan. Ensure that all fixing is at room temperature. Mix stevia and margarine until fluffy.

2. Put the eggs one at a time, and beat before you add the next one. Slowly add the whipping cream and flour, mixing between each addition.

3. Beat the mixture for approximately 30 seconds, then stirs- in the vanilla flavoring. Put the batter into your greased and floured tube pan; bake for 60 minutes.

Per serving: Calories: 249kcal; Fat: 4g; Carbs: 35g; Protein: 8g; Phosphorus: 24mg; Sodium: 192mg; Potassium: 120mg

140. Pineapple Cake

Preparation time: 30 minutes

Cooking time: 45 minutes

Servings: 6

Ingredients:

FOR THE BASE:

• 100 g of flour

• 2 eggs

• 200 g of stevia

• 8 g of vanilla yeast

FOR THE CREAM:

• 1 whole egg, 1 yolk

• 1 cup stevia

• 3 tablespoons flour

• 500 g semi-skimmed milk

• 250 g pineapple

• 200 g cream for desserts

• Grated lemon zest

Directions:

1. To prepare the base of the cake, you have to work the flour, stevia, and yeast until a homogeneous mixture. Bake at 160 degrees for

about 15 minutes. After baking, let the cake cool.

2. Meanwhile, prepare the cream. In a saucepan, place on low heat; beat a whole egg and the yolk with the stevia and flour.

3. Add the milk lukewarm previously brought to a boil, with 1/2 grated lemon zest.

4. Cook everything on a slow fire, stirring for about 4-5 minutes.

5. When the base has cooled, cut the upper part (2/3 sup.), pour on the bottom of the pineapple juice (from the can), then put the prepared cream and a layer of cream.

6. Finally, cover them with the mixture from crumbling the unused part of the cake (the smaller one) combined with the pineapple cut into small pieces.

7. Before serving, the cake must be in the fridge for 2 hours.

Per serving: Calories: 423kcal; Fat: 17g; Carbs: 61g; Protein: 10g; Phosphorus: 193mg; Sodium: 97mg; Potassium: 371mg

141. Strawberry Pie

Preparation time: 15 minutes

Cooking time: 20 minutes

Servings: 8

Ingredients:

For the Crust:

- 1 1/2 cups Graham cracker crumbs
- 5 tbsp oil at room temperature
- 4 tbsp. stevia

For the Pie:

- 1 1/2 tsp gelatin powder
- 3 tbsp cornstarch
- 2 cup stevia
- 5 cups sliced strawberries, divided
- 1 cup water

Directions:

1. For the crust: heat your oven to 375 F. Grease a pie pan. Combine the oil, crumbs, and stevia and press them into your pie pan.

2. Bake the crust for 10 to 15 minutes, until lightly browned. Take it out of the oven and let it cool completely.

3. For the pie, crush up a cup of strawberries. Combine the stevia, water, gelatin, and cornstarch using a small pot. Bring the mixture in the pot up to a boil, lower the heat, and simmer until it has thickened.

4. Add the crushed strawberries to the pot and let it simmer for another 5 minutes until the sauce has thickened up again. Set it off the heat and pour it into a bowl. Cool until it comes to room temperature.

5. Toss the remaining berries with the sauce to be well distributed, pour it into the pie crust, and spread it into an even layer. Refrigerate the pie until cold. It will take about 3 hours. Serve and enjoy!

Per serving: Calories: 265kcal; Fat: 7g; Carbs: 48g; Protein: 3g; Phosphorus: 44mg; Sodium: 143mg; Potassium: 183mg

142. Sweet Raspberry Candy

Preparation time: 5 minutes

Cooking time: 5 minutes

Servings: 12

Ingredients:

- 1/2 cup dried raspberries
- 3 tbsp Swerve
- 1/2 cup coconut oil
- 2 oz cacao oil
- 1/2 tsp vanilla

Directions:

1. Add cacao and coconut oil to a saucepan and melt over low heat. Remove from heat.

2. Grind the raspberries in a food processor.

3. Add sweetener and ground raspberries into the melted oil and coconut oil mixture and stir well.

4. Pour the mixture into the mini silicone candy molds and place them in the refrigerator until set.

5. Serve and enjoy.

Per serving: Calories: 103kcal; Fat: 11g; Carbs: 1g; Protein: 0.1g; Phosphorus: 95mg; Sodium: 45mg; Potassium: 123mg

143. Frozen Lemon Dessert

Preparation time: 15 minutes

Cooking time: 10 minutes

Servings: 6

Ingredients:

- 4 eggs separated
- 1/4 cup lemon juice
- 3 cup stevia
- 1 tbsp lemon peel, grated
- 2 cups vanilla wafers, crushed
- 1 cup whipping cream, whipped

Directions:

1. Beat the egg yolks until it becomes very thick. Slowly add stevia and beat each time you add. Put the lemon peel and lemon juice, and mix well.

2. Put the batter in your double boiler, then cook over boiling water, continually stirring until the mixture gets thick. Set aside to cool.

3. Mix the egg whites until stiff peaks. Fold the egg whites into the thick mixture once cooled.

4. Add whipped cream and fold in. Spread one and a half crumbs of the vanilla wafer in the bottom of a baking dish or freezer tray.

5. Scoop the lemon mixture and spread over the crumbs. Sprinkle the remaining vanilla wafer crumbs on top. Fridge for several hours until the mixture is firm.

Per serving: Calories: 205kcal; Fat: 6g; Carbs: 32g; Protein: 3g; Phosphorus: 33mg; Sodium: 97mg; Potassium: 69mg

144. Lemon Cake

Preparation time: 15 minutes

Cooking time: 1 hour & 20 minutes

Servings: 12

Ingredients:

- 2 cups oil
- 8 cups stevia
- 2 tsp grated lemon zest
- 1 tsp lemon extract
- 6 eggs

• 3 1/2 cups sifted all-purpose flour

Directions:

1. Preheat your oven to 350 degrees. Cream oil on low speed with an electric mixer until light and fluffy.

2. Slowly add in stevia and lemon zest; mix thoroughly. Add lemon extract and the eggs, one at a time, mixing after each addition.

3. Add flour gradually and mix well. Pour batter into a greased and floured pan. Bake for one hour and 20 minutes. You will know it is done when a toothpick inserted in the cake center comes out clean.

Per serving: Calories: 279kcal; Fat: 0g; Carbs: 34g; Protein: 10g; Phosphorus: 139mg; Sodium: 127mg; Potassium: 108mg

145. Frozen Fantasy

Preparation time: 15 minutes
Cooking time: 0 minutes
Servings: 4
Ingredients:

• 1 cup cranberry juice

• 1 cup fresh whole strawberries, washed and hulled

• 2 tbsp fresh lime juice

• 2 cup stevia

• 9 ice cubes

• a handful of strawberries for garnish

Directions:

1. Blend the cranberry juice, stevia, lime juice, and strawberries in a blender. Blend until the batter is smooth; add ice cubes and blend till

smooth. Pour into a glass and add strawberries to garnish.

Per serving: Calories: 100kcal; Fat: 0g; Carbs: 24g; Protein: 8g; Phosphorus: 129mg; Sodium: 3mg; Potassium: 109mg

146. Ribbon Cakes

Preparation time: 15 minutes
Cooking time: 30 minutes
Servings: 4
Ingredients:

• 3 cups unsoftened all-purpose flour

• 2 whole eggs

• 2 cup stevia

• 1 tsp baking powder

• jelly or jam like apricot jam/raspberry jelly

• 1 cup margarine or oil, softened

• 1 egg white

• 1/2 tsp vanilla

• 1 cup blackberry or plum

Directions:

1. Heat your oven to 375 degrees. Mix the stevia, flour, and baking powder in a bowl. Blend the oil using a pastry blender or your fingertips until the mixture looks like cornmeal.

2. Add egg white, eggs, and vanilla into the mixture and work into a stiff dough. Split the dough into two, with one part being twice the size of the other.

3. Spread about ¼ to ½ cups of flour on a board and roll out the bigger ball to approximately 1/8 inch thickness.

4. Put the rolled dough in a cookie pan and smoothen the edges. Spread the jelly/ jam on top. Roll out the leftover dough to the same thickness and cut it into half-inch wide strips.

5. Place the strips diagonally across the jam or jelly, half-inch apart. Put the stevia over the top of the dough and put it into the oven.

6. When the edges begin to brown after 20 minutes, remove and cut off about 3 inches around all the edges.

7. Take out the cut-off parts and place the pan back into the oven for approximately 10 minutes. Cut into 1-inch by 2-inches rectangles to give you seven dozen cookies.

Per serving: Calories: 106kcal; Fat: 0g; Carbs: 15g; Protein: 1g; Phosphorus: 27mg; Sodium: 65mg; Potassium: 17mg

147. Sandy Cake

Preparation time: 1 hour

Cooking time: 50 minutes

Servings: 6

Ingredients:

• 300 g starch

• 200 g oil

• 400 g stevia

• 3 whole eggs

• Half a sachet of yeast (8 g)

Directions:

1. Combine the starch, whole eggs, oil, and stevia in a bowl.

2. Add the well-dissolved yeast and mix until the mixture becomes uniform.

3. Pour the mixture into the pan and put it in the oven.

4. Cooking time 40-50 min., At 180 ° C.

Per serving: Calories: 589kcal; Fat: 30g; Carbs: 79g; Protein: 29g; Phosphorus: 80mg; Sodium: 54mg; Potassium: 203mg

148. Baked Egg Custard

Preparation time: 15 minutes

Cooking time: 30 minutes

Servings: 4

Ingredients:

• 2 eggs, medium-sized

• 1/4 cup 2% milk

• 3 tbsp stevia

• 1 tsp lemon extract or vanilla

• 1 tsp nutmeg

Directions:

1. Preheat your oven to 325 degrees. Mix all the fixing, and use an electric mixer to beat them for one minute until thoroughly mixed.

2. Pour the mixture into muffin pans or custard cups. Sprinkle a teaspoon of nutmeg on top. Bake for approx. 30 minutes.

3. To confirm that the cake is ready, insert a knife in the center of the custard, which should come out clean

Per serving: Calories: 70kcal; Fat: 0g; Carbs: 9g; Protein: 3g; Phosphorus: 42mg; Sodium: 34mg; Potassium: 30mg

149. Lemon Crispies

Preparation time: 15 minutes

Cooking time: 10 minutes

Servings: 12

Ingredients:

- 1 cup unsalted margarine or oil
- 1 egg
- 2 cup stevia
- 1 1/2 tsp lemon extract
- 1 1/2 cups all-purpose flour, sifted

Directions:

1. Preheat your oven to 375 degrees. Mix the oil and stevia. Add lemon extract and eggs to the mixture and beat until it becomes fluffy and light.

2. Add flour to the mixture and beat until smooth. Scoop the batter with a tablespoon and place it on an ungreased cookie sheet leaving at least a 2-inch space between the cookies.

3. Bake within 10 minutes or until the cookies turn brown around the edges. Allow the cookies to cool before you remove them from the cookie sheet

Per serving: Calories: 115kcal; Fat: 4g; Carbs: 12g; Protein: 2g; Phosphorus: 23mg; Sodium: 12mg; Potassium: 20mg

150. Spritz Cookies

Preparation time: 15 minutes

Cooking time: 8 minutes

Servings: 75 cookies

Ingredients:

- 5 cups all-purpose flour
- 2 cup + 4 tbsp stevia
- 2 cups oil - 2 eggs
- 1 tsp almond extract
- 2 tsp vanilla extract

Directions:

1. Preheat your oven to 400 degrees. Mix oil, flour, and stevia together. Put the vanilla almond extract and the eggs.

2. Mix the ingredients using a hand mixer at low speed. Put cookie batter into an ungreased baking sheet. Bake for about 8 minutes. Allow cooling before you serve.

Per serving: Calories: 172kcal; Fat: 0g; Carbs: 26g; Protein: 2g; Phosphorus: 22mg; Sodium: 56mg; Potassium: 29mg

30-Day Meal Plan

Days	Breakfast	Lunch	Dinner	Dessert
1	Cornbread With Southern Twist	Grilled Chicken	Korean Pear Salad	Chocolate Pie Shell
2	Breakfast Maple Sausage	Four-Ingredients Salmon Fillet	Breakfast Salad from Grains and Fruits	Whipped Cream Pound Cake
3	Very Berry Smoothie	Chili Mussels	Roasted Spatchcock Chicken	Sweet Raspberry Candy
4	Mexican Scrambled Eggs In Tortilla	Chicken Salad Balsamic	Poached Halibut In Mango Sauce	Frozen Fantasy
5	Raspberry Peach Breakfast Smoothie	Ground Turkey With Asparagus	Ground Beef And Rice Soup	Strawberry Tiramisu
6	Fast Microwave Egg Scramble	Oven-Fried Southern-Style Catfish	Fruity Zucchini Salad	Fruit Crunch
7	Egg And Veggie Muffins	Cucumber Couscous Salad	Grilled Chicken With Pineapple & Veggies	Baked Egg Custard
8	Feta Mint Omelet	Enjoyable Green Lettuce And Bean Medley	Herbed Vegetable Trout	Small Chocolate Cakes
9	Sausage Cheese Bake Omelet	Chicken Meatloaf With Veggies	Grapes Jicama Salad	Frozen Lemon Dessert
10	French Toast With Applesauce	Asparagus Shrimp Linguini	Traditional Black Bean Chili	Pineapple Cake
11	Mango Lassi Smoothie	Sardine Fish Cakes	Ground Chicken With Basil	Lemon Crispies

12	Raspberry Overnight Porridge	Carrot Jicama Salad	Broiled Shrimp	Ribbon Cakes
13	Buckwheat And Grapefruit Porridge	Ground Turkey With Veggies	Italian Cucumber Salad	Spritz Cookies
14	Grandma's Pancake Special	Broiled Salmon Fillets	Chinese Tempeh Stir Fry	Chocolate Beet Cake
15	American Blueberry Pancakes	Tuna Macaroni Salad	Grilled Chicken Pizza	Chocolate Muffins
16	Spicy Corn Bread	Hawaiian Chicken Salad	Salmon Baked In Foil With Fresh Thyme	Jeweled Cookies
17	Mexican Style Burritos	Roasted Chicken Breast	Saucy Fish Dill	Strawberry Pie
18	Summer Veggie Omelet	Grilled Lemony Cod	Panzanella Salad	Fruit Salad
19	Pasta With Indian Lentils	Green Tuna Salad	Chicken Breast And Bok Choy	Sandy Cake
20	Breakfast Smoothie	Couscous Salad	Fish En' Papillote	Lemon Cake
21	Egg And Veggie Muffins	Curried Chicken With Cauliflower	Fish Chili With Lentils	Strawberry Tiramisu
22	Feta Mint Omelet	Haddock &Oiled Leeks	Butterscotch Apple Salad	Fruit Crunch
23	Sausage Cheese Bake Omelet	Tuna Casserole	Creamy Chicken	Baked Egg Custard
24	Cornbread With Southern Twist	Sesame Cucumber Salad	Spanish Cod In Sauce	Small Chocolate Cakes
25	Breakfast Maple Sausage	Chicken &Veggie Casserole	Thai Cucumber Salad	Chocolate Pie Shell

26	Very Berry Smoothie	Citrus Glazed Salmon	Salmon & Pesto Salad	Whipped Cream Pound Cake
27	Mexican Scrambled Eggs In Tortilla	Farmer's Salad	Beer Pork Ribs	Sweet Raspberry Candy
28	Grandma's Pancake Special	Chestnut Noodle Salad	Oregon Tuna Patties	Lemon Crispies
29	American Blueberry Pancakes	Red And Green Grapes Chicken Salad With Curry	Grated Carrot Salad With Lemon-Dijon Vinaigrette	Ribbon Cakes
30	Spicy Corn Bread	Spiced Honey Salmon	Cucumber Salad	Spritz Cookies

Index

Mango Lassi Smoothie; 27
Marinated Berries; 73
Mediterranean Vegetable Soup; 68
Mexican Scrambled Eggs In Tortilla; 25
Mexican Style Burritos; 21
Nutmeg Chicken Soup; 65
Oregon Tuna Patties; 58
Oven-Fried Southern Style Catfish; 59
Oxtail Soup; 68
Panzanella Salad; 42
Paprika Pork Soup; 70
Pasta With Indian Lentils; 27
Pecan Caramel Corn; 77
Pineapple Cake; 84
Poached Halibut In Mango Sauce; 58
Popcorn With Sugar And Spice; 78
Raspberry Overnight Porridge; 22
Raspberry Peach Breakfast Smoothie; 21
Red And Green Grapes Chicken Salad With Curry; 49
Ribbon Cakes; 87
Roasted Asparagus With Pine Nuts; 78
Roasted Chicken Breast; 52
Roasted Radishes; 80
Roasted Spatchcock Chicken; 49
Rosemary And White Bean Dip; 79
Salmon & Pesto Salad; 40
Salmon And Green Beans; 35
Salmon Baked In Foil With Fresh Thyme; 57
Sandy Cake; 88
Sardine Fish Cakes; 62
Saucy Fish Dill; 56
Sausage Cheese Bake Omelet; 28

Sautéed Green Beans; 32
Sautéed Spicy Cabbage; 78
Seasoned Green Beans; 38
Sesame Cucumber Salad; 43
Shrimp Spread With Crackers; 75
Small Chocolate Cakes; 81
Spanish Cod In Sauce; 57
Spanish Rice; 37
Spiced Honey Salmon; 63
Spicy Chicken Soup; 72
Spicy Corn Bread; 22
Spicy Crab Dip; 74
Spicy Guacamole; 79
Spritz Cookies; 89
Squash And Turmeric Soup; 65
Strawberry Pie; 85
Strawberry Tiramisu; 81
Summer Veggie Omelet; 23
Sweet And Spicy Tortilla Chips; 75
Sweet Raspberry Candy; 86
Thai Cucumber Salad; 41
Thai Spiced Halibut; 36
Traditional Black Bean Chili; 35
Tuna Casserole; 61
Tuna Macaroni Salad; 44
Turkey & Lemon-Grass Soup; 69
Vegetable Fried Rice; 33
Vegetable Rolls; 76
Veggie Snack; 73
Very Berry Smoothie; 27
Whipped Cream Pound Cake; 84
Wild Rice Asparagus Soup; 70
Zesty Green Beans With Almonds; 31

Conversion Chart

Volume Equivalents (Liquid)

US Standard	US Standard (ounces)	Metric (approximate)
2 tablespoons	1 fl. oz.	30 mL
¼ cup	2 fl. oz.	60 mL
½ cup	4 fl. oz.	120 mL
1 cup	8 fl. oz.	240 mL
1½ cups	12 fl. oz.	355 mL
2 cups or 1 pint	16 fl. oz.	475 mL
4 cups or 1 quart	32 fl. oz.	1 L
1 gallon	128 fl. oz.	4 L

Volume Equivalents (Dry)

US Standard	Metric (approximate)
⅛ teaspoon	0.5 mL
¼ teaspoon	1 mL
½ teaspoon	2 mL
¾ teaspoon	4 mL
1 teaspoon	5 mL
1 tablespoon	15 mL
¼ cup	59 mL
⅓ cup	79 mL
½ cup	118 mL
⅔ cup	156 mL
¾ cup	177 mL
1 cup	235 mL
2 cups or 1 pint	475 mL
3 cups	700 mL
4 cups or 1 quart	1 L

Oven Temperatures

Fahrenheit (F)	Celsius (C) (approximate)
250°F	120°C
300°F	150°C
325°F	165°C
350°F	180°C
375°F	190°C
400°F	200°C
425°F	220°C
450°F	230°C

Weight Equivalents

US Standard	Metric (approximate)
1 tablespoon	15 g
½ ounce	15 g
1 ounce	30 g
2 ounces	60 g
4 ounces	115 g
8 ounces	225 g
12 ounces	340 g
16 ounces or 1 pound	455 g

Conclusion

Your kidneys play an essential role in your physical well-being. These organs are in charge of a variety of tasks, including the removal of bodily waste and the production of hormones. As a result, taking care of the kidneys can be a high priority for your well-being.

The only thing you can do to keep your kidneys safe is to live an active, health-conscious lifestyle.

If you have a severe health problem that puts you at risk for kidney injury or cancer, you can work closely with the doctor to keep an eye out for symptoms of kidney failure.

The kidney-friendly foods mentioned in this book are excellent options for those on a renal diet.

Please consult a healthcare professional on your dietary preferences and guarantee that you practice the proper diet for your specific needs.

Dietary restrictions differ based on the type and severity of kidney damage and the medical procedures used, such as drugs or dialysis.

Although adhering to a renal diet may seem restricting, many tasty items can be included in a nutritious, well-balanced, kidney-friendly meal schedule.

One deficiency in phosphorous, Protein, and Sodium; is a renal diet. Each patient's body is different, so each patient needs to collaborate with a renal dietitian to create a diet customized to the patient's needs. A renal diet often highlights the value of eating high-quality Protein and limiting liquids.

For patients with renal failure, too much salt may be dangerous since their kidneys cannot properly remove extra fluid and Sodium; from the body. As fluid and Sodium; build up in the bloodstream and tissues, they can cause Edema, heart failure, high blood pressure, etc. Therefore, individuals with kidney disease must follow a kidney-friendly diet to enjoy a healthy life.

Made in United States
Troutdale, OR
03/04/2024

18209764R00058